WeightWatchers®
COOK SMART soups

Easy, delicious soup recipes for every occasion

SIMON & SCHUSTER
A CBS COMPANY

First published in Great Britain by Simon & Schuster UK Ltd, 2010
A CBS Company

Copyright © 2010, Weight Watchers International, Inc.
Simon & Schuster UK Ltd, First Floor, 222 Gray's Inn Road, London WC1X 8HB

Weight Watchers Publications Team: Jane Griffiths, Fiona Smith, Erica Collins and Philip Newton.

A selection of recipes appear courtesy of weightwatchers.co.uk. For more information about Weight Watchers Online visit www.weightwatchers.co.uk

Recipes written by: Sue Ashworth, Sue Beveridge, Tamsin Burnett-Hall, Cas Clarke, Siân Davies, Roz Denny, Nicola Graimes, Becky Johnson, Kim Morphew, Joy Skipper, Penny Stephens and Wendy Veale.

Photography by: Iain Bagwell, Steve Baxter, Steve Lee and Juliet Piddington
Design and typesetting by Tiger Media Ltd
Printed and bound in China

A CIP catalogue for this book is available from the British Library

ISBN 978-1-84737-855-2

1 3 5 7 9 10 8 6 4 2

Pictured on the front cover: Minestrone Soup p55, Jaipur-style Dahl Soup p56, Spicy Pork Meatball Soup p124, Quick Tomato Soup p65.
Pictured on the back cover: Broccoli Soup with Cheese Clouds p148, Chinese Shredded Vegetable Soup p17, Noodle Bar Soup p150, Sweet Potato and Chilli Soup p108.
Pictured on the introduction: Quick Tomato Soup p65, Noodle Bar Soup p150, Root and Orange Soup p30, Manhattan Seafood Soup p88.

 POINTS ® value logo: You'll find this easy to read *POINTS* value logo on every recipe throughout this book. The logo represents the number of *POINTS* values per serving each recipe contains. Weight Watchers offers you a healthy and sustainable way to lose weight. For more information about Weight Watchers call 08457 123 000.

V This symbol denotes a vegetarian recipe and assumes that, where relevant, free range eggs, vegetarian cheese, vegetarian virtually fat free fromage frais, vegetarian low fat crème fraîche and vegetarian low fat yogurts are used. Virtually fat free fromage frais, low fat crème fraîche and low fat yogurts may contain traces of gelatine so they are not always vegetarian. Please check the labels.

✱ This symbol denotes a dish that can be frozen.

Recipe notes
Egg size: Medium, unless otherwise stated.
All fruits and vegetables: Medium sized, unless otherwise stated.
Raw eggs: Only the freshest eggs should be used. Pregnant women, the elderly and children should avoid recipes with eggs that are not fully cooked or raw.
Stock: Stock cubes used in recipes, unless otherwise stated. These should be prepared according to packet instructions.
Recipe timings: These are approximate and meant to be guidelines. Please note that the preparation time includes all the steps up to and following the main cooking time(s).
Low fat spread: Where a recipe states to use a low fat spread, a light spread with a fat content of no less than 38% should be used.

Contents

Introduction

Welcome to Weight Watchers *Cook Smart Soups*, full of fantastic recipes. There's nothing like a bowl of fresh, home-made soup; it's the perfect meal – satisfying, warming, filling and delicious. It's easy too – just a little chopping and cooking. Try out the recipes in this book and surprise your friends and family.

There are over 100 soup recipes in this book, many suitable for vegetarians. They cover a variety of styles, from light and quick broths to hearty, filling chowders and everything in between. Using fresh ingredients as well as everyday items from your store cupboard, soups are a great choice for a meal any time.

About Weight Watchers

For more than 40 years Weight Watchers has been helping people around the world to lose weight using a long term sustainable approach. Weight Watchers, successful weight loss system is based on four tried and trusted principles:

- Eating healthily
- Being more active
- Adjusting behaviour to help weight loss
- Getting support in weekly meetings.

Our unique **POINTS** system empowers you to manage your food plan and make wise recipe choices for a healthier, happier you.

Basic Ingredients

Milk

Always use skimmed milk, rather than whole or semi-skimmed, unless otherwise stated in the recipe.

Eggs

Use medium sized eggs, unless otherwise stated in the recipe. Always bring eggs to room temperature before using. A cold egg won't whisk well and the shell will crack if placed in hot water.

Fats and Oils

The majority of recipes use low fat cooking spray rather than oil. Low fat cooking spray can be either olive oil or sunflower oil based. Try both and see which you prefer. Generally, low fat spread with a fat content no less than 38% is used in recipes rather than butter.

Cheese and Yogurt

Any cheese used in these recipes is low fat Cheddar, low fat soft cheese or virtually fat free fromage frais. Some recipes use yogurt. Always choose either 0% fat Greek yogurt or low fat natural. All of these products are easy to find in a supermarket.

Fruit and vegetables

Make sure your family eats plenty of fruit and vegetables, preferably at least five portions a day. Many of these soup recipes are based on vegetables, providing a wonderfully tasty way to enjoy vegetables. Look for what is in season and use up a glut by making soup and freezing it. Filling up on fruit and vegetables will also stop you from feeling hungry, so you are less likely to snack on fatty and sugary foods.

Planning Ahead

When you're going around the supermarket it is tempting to pick up foods you like and put them in your trolley without thinking about how you will use them. So, a good plan is to decide what dishes you want to cook before you go shopping, check your store cupboard ingredients and make a list of what you need. You'll save time by not drifting aimlessly around the supermarket picking up what you fancy. You might even have time for a cup of tea or coffee.

Store Cupboard Suggestions

bay leaves

borlotti beans, canned

bouquet garni

butter beans, canned

chick peas, canned

chilli (flakes, powder)

Chinese cooking wine

cornflour

couscous

creamed coconut

fish sauce, Thai

flageolet beans, canned

flour, plain

garlic cloves

ginger

haricot beans, canned

herbs, dried (mixed, oregano, thyme, etc.)

honey, runny

kaffir lime leaves

kidney beans, canned

lemongrass

lemons

lentils (Puy, red, brown and yellow)

low fat coconut milk

low fat cooking spray

mayonnaise, extra light

mushrooms, dried

mussels, canned

mustard (Dijon or wholegrain)

noodles (rice and egg)

oil (vegetable)

passata

pasta

pearl barley

peas (frozen)

peppercorns

prawns, frozen

rice (easy cook, basmati and risotto)

saffron

salt (sea salt or low sodium)

seafood, mixed (frozen)

seeds (caraway, fennel, cumin)

sherry (dry and medium)

soy sauce, light

spices, ground (coriander, cumin, Chinese 5 spice, Thai 7 spice, turmeric, paprika, cinnamon, ginger, nutmeg, cayenne pepper, curry powder)

star anise

stock cubes (vegetable, chicken and beef)

sugar (muscovado)

sweetcorn (canned, frozen and creamed)

Tabasco sauce

Thai curry paste

tomato juice

tomato purée

tomatoes, canned

vinegar (balsamic, white wine, rice)

water chestnuts, canned

Worcestershire sauce

yellow split peas

Zero *POINTS* Value Soups

The recipes in this chapter show just how filling soup can be, but without adding to your *POINTS* allowance. From light Chinese Shredded Vegetable to autumnal Root and Orange and from Hot Red Pepper to Roasted Pumpkin, there is something here for everyone.

Fill up on soup without filling up on *POINTS* values

Hot Red Pepper Soup

This is a very intense and fiery, deep red soup – serve with a tablespoon of low fat natural yogurt per person to cool things down, for an extra ½ **POINTS** value per serving.

Serves 4

6 red peppers, halved and de-seeded
low fat cooking spray
2 onions, chopped finely
1 tablespoon fennel seeds (optional)
3 garlic cloves, crushed
1 red chilli, de-seeded and chopped finely
   (optional)
400 g can chopped tomatoes
1.2 litres (2 pints) vegetable stock
2 tablespoons Worcestershire sauce
2 teaspoons Tabasco sauce
salt and freshly ground black pepper
a small bunch of fresh basil, chopped roughly,
   to garnish

0 **POINTS** values per serving
0 **POINTS** values per recipe

C 120 **calories** per serving

Takes **15 minutes** to prepare,
25 minutes to cook

V if not using Worcestershire sauce

✱ not recommended

1 Preheat the grill and put the peppers on the grill pan skin side-up. Grill for 5–10 minutes, until blistered and blackened and then place in a plastic bag, wrap and leave to cool.

2 Meanwhile heat a large, non stick saucepan and spray with the cooking spray. Stir fry the onions with the fennel seeds, if using, for 5 minutes, adding a little water if necessary to prevent them from sticking.

3 When the peppers are cool enough to handle, peel them and add the flesh to the onions along with all the other ingredients except the basil. Bring to the boil and simmer for 10 minutes.

4 Liquidise the soup in batches using a blender or hand held blender and return to the pan to warm through.

5 Check the seasoning then serve in warmed bowls garnished with the basil.

Variation For a less spicy version, just omit the chilli and Tabasco sauce.

Courgette and Mint Soup

A tasty way to enjoy courgettes in this great summertime soup.

Serves 4
low fat cooking spray
1 large onion, sliced finely
1 kg (2 lb 4 oz) courgettes, chopped roughly
1.2 litres (2 pints) vegetable stock
a bunch of fresh mint, chopped
salt and freshly ground black pepper

1 Spray a large, non stick saucepan with the cooking spray and stir fry the onion for 5 minutes, until softened, adding a little water if necessary to prevent it from sticking.

2 Add the courgettes, stock, seasoning and half the mint.

3 Bring to the boil and then simmer for 10 minutes, until the courgettes are tender. Add most of the remaining mint, reserving a little for garnishing.

4 Liquidise the soup in batches using a blender or hand held blender and return to the pan to warm through.

5 Check the seasoning and then serve in warmed bowls garnished with the reserved mint and a grinding of black pepper.

0 POINTS values per serving
0 POINTS values per recipe

C **61 calories** per serving

Takes **10 minutes** to prepare,
20 minutes to cook

V

* recommended

Carrot and Coriander Soup

This classic is transformed by the fresh coriander.

Serves 4

low fat cooking spray
1 large onion, sliced thinly
1 kg (2 lb 4 oz) carrots, peeled and chopped roughly
1.2 litres (2 pints) chicken or vegetable stock
1 packet fresh coriander (including roots), rinsed, drained and chopped
salt and freshly ground black pepper

1 Heat a large, non stick saucepan and spray with the cooking spray. Stir fry the onion for 5 minutes until softened, adding a little water if necessary to prevent it from sticking.

2 Add the carrots, stock, the chopped roots and stalks of the coriander and seasoning.

3 Bring to the boil and then simmer for 15 minutes until the carrots are tender. Add the rest of the chopped coriander.

4 Liquidise the soup in batches using a blender or hand held blender and return to the pan to warm through.

5 Check the seasoning and serve in warmed bowls garnished with the reserved coriander.

0 *POINTS* values per serving
0 *POINTS* values per recipe

C **96 calories** per serving

Takes **10 minutes** to prepare, **20 minutes** to cook

V if using vegetable stock

✳ not recommended

Variation This soup is also very good made with parsnips instead of carrots, for 2½ *POINTS* values per serving.

Red Hot Tomato and Beetroot Soup

0 POINTS VALUE

A delicious blend of tomatoes and beetroot 'warmed up' with a hint of cumin, this wintery soup makes you glow just by looking at it. Serve with a tablespoon of low fat natural yogurt per person, for an additional ½ **POINTS** value per serving. Perfect for entertaining.

Serves 4

low fat cooking spray
1 large onion, chopped
1 garlic clove, crushed
225 g (8 oz) raw beetroot, peeled and grated or finely sliced
225 g (8 oz) fresh tomatoes, skinned and roughly chopped
300 ml (½ pint) tomato juice
1 tablespoon tomato purée
1 teaspoon ground cumin
½ teaspoon ground cinnamon
600 ml (1 pint) hot vegetable stock
salt and freshly ground black pepper

0 **POINTS** values per serving
0 **POINTS** values per recipe

C 72 **calories** per serving

Takes **10 minutes** to prepare, **30 minutes** to cook

V

✱ recommended

1 Heat a large, lidded, non stick saucepan and spray with the cooking spray. Add the onion, garlic and beetroot. Cover and cook gently for 10 minutes, shaking the pan occasionally and adding a little water if necessary to prevent them from sticking.

2 Add the tomatoes, tomato juice, tomato purée, spices and stock. Cover and bring to the boil.

3 Reduce the heat and simmer gently for 15 minutes or until the vegetables are tender. Season well.

4 Liquidise the soup in batches using a blender or hand held blender, until very smooth, and return to the pan to warm through. Adjust the seasoning to taste.

5 Ladle into warmed bowls to serve.

Tip For added convenience, replace the fresh tomatoes and tomato juice with a 400 g can of chopped tomatoes. The **POINTS** values will remain the same.

Variation For a fruity note, add 1 medium cooking apple, peeled, cored and chopped, at step 2. Core and finely slice a red skinned dessert apple to garnish the soup too, for an extra ½ **POINTS** value per serving.

Satisfying Vegetable Soup

This soup is full of flavour and nutritious so tuck in.

Serves 4

low fat cooking spray
1 onion
2 leeks, chopped finely
2 garlic cloves, crushed
400 g can chopped tomatoes
2 carrots, peeled and diced finely
175 g (6 oz) white cabbage, shredded thinly
1.2 litres (2 pints) hot vegetable stock
350 g (12 oz) courgettes, diced finely
100 g (3½ oz) green beans, quartered lengthwise
1 tablespoon balsamic vinegar
salt and freshly ground black pepper
a handful of chopped flat leafed parsley, to garnish

1 Heat a large, non stick saucepan and spray with the cooking spray. Sauté the onion and leeks for 5 minutes until softened, adding a little water if necessary to prevent them from sticking.

2 Add the garlic, tomatoes, carrots and cabbage. Mix everything together, pour the hot stock over and simmer for 30 minutes.

3 Add the courgettes, beans, seasoning and vinegar and cook for a further 5 minutes.

4 Serve in warmed bowls sprinkled with chopped parsley.

0 POINTS values per serving
0 POINTS values per recipe

C   **100 calories** per serving

Takes **15 minutes** to prepare, **40 minutes** to cook

V

✱   not recommended

Tip Use 2 teaspoons of garlic purée as a convenient alternative to fresh garlic, for the same **POINTS** values.

Chinese Shredded Vegetable Soup

This light, speedy soup makes a perfect stop gap when you're feeling hungry.

Serves 4

850 ml (1½ pints) hot vegetable stock
½ teaspoon Chinese 5 spice powder
2 tablespoons light soy sauce
2 tablespoons fresh coriander, chopped
**2 generous handfuls of fresh or frozen zero *POINTS* value stir fry
  vegetables**
salt and freshly ground black pepper

1 Pour the stock into a large saucepan. Add the Chinese 5 spice
   powder and bring up to the boil.

2 Add the soy sauce, coriander and vegetables. Simmer for 5 minutes.

3 Check the seasoning and serve at once in warmed bowls.

0 *POINTS* values per serving
0 *POINTS* values per recipe

C **24 calories** per serving

Takes **5 minutes** to prepare,
10 minutes to cook

V

* recommended

Variation To transform this soup into a light supper, add 125 g (4½ oz)
flat rice noodles with the vegetables, for 1½ *POINTS* values per serving.

Roasted Pumpkin Soup

A fantastic soup for autumn, with a beautiful orange colour. Roasting creates a more intense flavour and the Chinese 5 spice powder gives it added warmth. Serve with 1 tablespoon of low fat natural yogurt per person, for ½ **POINTS** value per serving.

Serves 4

low fat cooking spray
6 shallots, unpeeled and cut in half
2 garlic cloves, unpeeled and crushed
750 g (1 lb 10 oz) pumpkin, peeled, de-seeded and chopped roughly
2 teaspoons Chinese 5 spice powder
1.2 litres (2 pints) vegetable stock
salt and freshly ground black pepper
a small bunch of fresh chives, chopped, to garnish

0 POINTS values per serving
0 POINTS values per recipe

C **46 calories** per serving

Takes **20 minutes** to prepare, **40 minutes** to cook

V

✳ recommended

1 Preheat the oven to Gas Mark 7/220°C/fan oven 200°C.

2 Spray a large roasting tray with the cooking spray. Add the shallots, garlic and pumpkin. Toss with the seasoning and Chinese 5 spice powder.

3 Roast in the oven for 30 minutes, stirring occasionally, until the vegetables are softened and slightly charred. Remove from the oven and set aside to cool.

4 When cool enough to handle, peel the skins from the shallots and garlic and discard, then transfer everything to a large saucepan and add the stock. Bring to the boil and simmer for 10 minutes.

5 Liquidise the soup in batches using a blender or hand held blender and return to the pan to warm through.

6 Check the seasoning and serve in warmed bowls with a scattering of chives to granish.

Curried Aubergine Soup

If you never know what to do with aubergines, try this spicy soup. Easy to make, it is a great way to use up these colourful vegetables.

Serves 4

1 onion, chopped
1 garlic clove, crushed
1 tablespoon medium curry powder
1 aubergine, diced
225 g (8 oz) carrots, peeled and diced
850 ml (1½ pints) vegetable stock
400 g can chopped tomatoes
salt and freshly ground black pepper
1 tablespoon chopped fresh coriander, to garnish

0 POINTS values per serving
0 POINTS values per recipe

C **80 calories** per serving

Takes **15 minutes** to prepare,
30 minutes to cook

V

✳ recommended

1 Place the onion, garlic, curry powder, aubergine and carrots in a large saucepan. Add the stock, chopped tomatoes and seasoning.

2 Bring to the boil and then simmer for 25 minutes, until the aubergine is very pulpy.

3 Liquidise the soup in batches using a blender or hand held blender, so the texture of the soup is not entirely smooth, and return to the pan to warm through.

4 Serve in warmed bowls garnished with the coriander.

Easy Vegetable Broth

Keep a batch of this soup in the fridge and when you're hungry, simply enjoy a bowlful without using any *POINTS* values.

Serves 4

1 red onion, chopped finely
225 g (8 oz) carrots, peeled and diced
3 celery sticks, sliced thinly
175 g (6 oz) swede, chopped finely
1.2 litres (2 pints) vegetable or chicken stock
1 tablespoon tomato purée
400 g can chopped tomatoes
salt and freshly ground black pepper
2 tablespoons chopped fresh mixed herbs, such
  as chives, parsley, basil and oregano, to garnish

0 *POINTS* values per serving
0 *POINTS* values per recipe

C **85 calories** per serving

Takes **15 minutes** to prepare,
30 minutes to cook

V if using vegetable stock

* recommended

1 Place the onion, carrots, celery, swede, stock, tomato purée and chopped tomatoes in a large saucepan and bring to the boil.

2 Reduce the heat and simmer gently for 25 minutes, until the vegetables are very tender.

3 Season to taste and stir in the fresh herbs just before serving in warmed bowls.

Tip Take time to chop the vegetables finely to enable some of the vegetables to break down during cooking and thicken the soup. This way you'll have a chunky soup that won't be too watery.

Smooth Gazpacho

Here's a quick and easy version of this lovely refreshing soup. It's usually served chilled but can be gently warmed, if you prefer.

Serves 2

450 g (1 lb) ripe tomatoes, chopped roughly
½ cucumber, peeled and chopped roughly
1 small red onion, chopped roughly
1 garlic clove, crushed
1 red pepper, de-seeded and chopped roughly
1 tablespoon wine vinegar
a small bunch of parsley, basil or mint, chopped roughly (with a little chopped finely for garnishing)
salt and freshly ground black pepper
a few ice cubes, to serve

0 POINTS values per serving
0 POINTS values per recipe

C **96 calories** per serving

Takes **10 minutes** + **30 minutes** chilling

V

✳ not recommended

1 Liquidise all the ingredients, apart from the ice cubes and seasoning, using a blender or hand held blender, then pour into a bowl. (If you prefer a smooth soup, strain it by pushing through a sieve.) Season.

2 Chill for at least 30 minutes.

3 Stir and serve with a few ice cubes in each soup bowl. Garnish each bowl with the finely chopped herbs.

Cabbage, Pepper and Leek Soup

This colourful medley of vegetables is full of flavour and a quick filler when you are hungry.

Serves 4

1 litre (1¾ pints) hot vegetable stock

a bunch of spring onions, trimmed and sliced finely

1 carrot, peeled and cut into fine strips

1 teaspoon Thai 7 spice seasoning

1 leek, shredded finely

1 small courgette, shredded finely

1 red or yellow pepper, de-seeded and shredded finely

50 g (1¾ oz) Savoy or white cabbage, shredded coarsely

a pinch of dried red chilli flakes (optional)

salt and freshly ground black pepper

1 tablespoon chopped fresh coriander or parsley, to garnish

1 Pour the stock into a large, lidded saucepan and add the spring onions and carrot.

2 Bring to the boil, then cover and reduce the heat. Simmer for 5 minutes.

3 Add the Thai 7 spice seasoning, leek, courgette, pepper and cabbage. Add the red chilli flakes, if using, replace the lid and bring back to a simmer. Simmer for a further 5 minutes.

4 Season to taste, then ladle the soup into warmed bowls and serve, garnished with chopped fresh coriander or parsley.

0 POINTS values per serving
0 POINTS values per recipe

C **46 calories** per serving

Takes **10 minutes** to prepare,
15 minutes to cook

V

✱ not recommended

Butternut Squash Soup

This delicious zero **POINTS** value soup couldn't be simpler to make.

Serves 2

1 small butternut squash, peeled, de-seeded and chopped
1 onion, chopped
600 ml (1 pint) hot vegetable stock
salt and freshly ground black pepper

1 Put the squash and onion into a large saucepan and add the stock.

2 Bring up to the boil, then reduce the heat and simmer for about 20 minutes until the squash is tender.

3 Liquidise the soup in batches using a blender or hand held blender and return to the pan to warm through.

4 Season to taste then serve in warmed bowls.

0 POINTS values per serving
0 POINTS values per recipe

C **155 calories** per serving

Takes **10 minutes** to prepare, **20 minutes** to cook

V

* recommended

Tip For four servings, use a medium to large butternut squash, a large onion and 850 ml (1½ pints) vegetable stock. The **POINTS** values will remain the same.

Variations When in season, try making this soup with pumpkin instead of squash, for the same **POINTS** values per serving.

For a spicy flavour, try adding a good pinch of ground cumin and ground coriander to the soup with the stock, for no extra **POINTS** values. Garnish with chopped fresh coriander or parsley.

Celery and Tomato Soup

The popular combination of celery and tomato is wonderful in this soup. It's a tasty and clever way to deal with those hungry moments.

Serves 4

low fat cooking spray
4 celery sticks, chopped finely
1 onion, chopped finely
1 carrot, peeled and grated coarsely
1 large garlic clove, chopped
420 g can chopped tomatoes
500 ml (18 fl oz) vegetable stock
salt and freshly ground black pepper

To garnish
1–2 tablespoons chopped fresh parsley
a few small celery leaves

0 POINTS values per serving
0 POINTS values per recipe

C **45 calories** per serving

Takes **5 minutes** to prepare,
25 minutes to cook

V

✳ recommended

1 Heat a large, lidded, non stick saucepan and spray with the cooking spray. Lightly cook the celery, onion, carrot and garlic, then add 6 tablespoons of water.

2 Cover and cook gently for 10 minutes, shaking the pan occasionally.

3 Stir in the chopped tomatoes and then the stock.

4 Season and bring to the boil. Reduce the heat and simmer for a further 10 minutes, or until the celery is tender. Check the seasoning.

5 Ladle the soup into warmed bowls and sprinkle with the chopped parsley and the small celery leaves.

Variation You can turn this into a spicy Mexican style soup by substituting a chopped green pepper for the celery and adding ½ –1 tablespoon mild chilli powder and ¼ teaspoon ground cumin in step 1, for no extra **POINTS** values.

Roast Tomato and Garlic Soup

An intensely flavoured soup that's thick, rich and satisfying.

Serves 2

500 g (1 lb 2 oz) ripe tomatoes, quartered

2 red onions, cut into wedges

1 bulb of garlic, divided into cloves but
  unpeeled

1 red pepper, de-seeded and quartered

low fat cooking spray

300 ml (½ pint) hot vegetable stock

1 tablespoon balsamic vinegar

1 tablespoon Worcestershire sauce

salt and freshly ground black pepper

a small bunch of fresh parsley, chopped roughly,
  to garnish (optional)

---

0 *POINTS* values per serving
0 *POINTS* values per recipe

C   70 calories per serving

Takes **15 minutes** to prepare,
45 minutes to cook

V   if not using Worcestershire sauce

✱   recommended

1 Preheat the oven to Gas Mark 7/220°C/fan oven 200°C.

2 Put the tomatoes, onions, garlic and red pepper into a large roasting tin. Season and spray with the cooking spray. Roast for 45 minutes, until the vegetables begin to char at the edges.

3 Remove the vegetables from the oven and allow to cool for a few minutes. Squeeze the garlic cloves out of their skins and liquidise in batches using a blender or hand held blender with all the other roasted vegetables, stock, vinegar and Worcestershire sauce.

4 Tip the purée into a saucepan and heat through for a few minutes.

5 Season and serve in warmed bowls scattered with the parsley, if using.

Chilli Soup

Serve with 1 teaspoon half fat crème fraîche per person, for an extra 2 **POINTS** values per serving.

Serves 4

1–2 fresh green chillies, de-seeded and chopped finely
150 g (5½ oz) green beans, each chopped into three
150 g (5½ oz) broccoli, broken into florets
150 g (5½ oz) dark green cabbage leaves, shredded
1 green pepper, de-seeded and chopped
1 onion, chopped
2 garlic cloves, chopped
850 ml (1½ pints) vegetable stock
salt and freshly ground black pepper
a few chopped chives, to garnish (optional)

0 **POINTS** values per serving
0 **POINTS** values per recipe

C 55 calories per serving

Takes **15 minutes** to prepare, **20 minutes** to cook

V

✳ not recommended

1 Place all the ingredients except the chives in a large saucepan and bring to the boil.

2 Turn down the heat and simmer for 15–20 minutes, until the vegetables are tender.

3 Liquidise the soup in batches using a blender or hand held blender and return to the pan to warm through.

4 Check the seasoning and serve in warmed bowls, garnished with chives, if using.

Root and Orange Soup

This colourful soup is great on a cool autumn day and is zero **POINTS** values.

Serves 6

500 g (1 lb 2 oz) carrots, peeled and sliced
1 small swede, diced
2 red onions, chopped
1 garlic clove, crushed
1.5 litres (2¾ pints) hot vegetable stock
1 tablespoon tomato purée
1 tablespoon balsamic vinegar
finely grated zest and juice of an orange
1 tablespoon chopped fresh parsley or
  chives, plus extra to garnish
salt and freshly ground black pepper

0 POINTS values per serving
½ POINTS value per recipe

C 75 calories per serving

Takes **15 minutes** to prepare,
20 minutes to cook

V

✶ recommended

1 Put the carrots, swede, onions, garlic, stock, tomato purée and balsamic vinegar into a large saucepan and stir well. Bring up to the boil, then reduce the heat to low and simmer gently for 15–20 minutes, or until the vegetables are tender.

2 Leave the soup chunky or liquidise in batches using a blender or hand held blender, for a smoother consistency.

3 Return to the pan and stir in the orange zest and juice together with the parsley or chives. Reheat gently and season to taste.

4 Ladle the soup into warmed bowls and garnish with the extra chopped parsley or chives.

Tip For a special garnish, top each portion with a tablespoon of low fat yogurt, the parsley or chives and a little more grated orange zest, for ½ **POINTS** value per serving.

Variation Ring the changes with lemon zest and juice instead of orange, and change the vegetables according to their availability – for instance, use spring onions or shallots instead of red onions. The **POINTS** values will remain the same.

Celery and Leek Soup

A delicious soup with an unusual flavour from the caraway seeds.

Serves 4
350 g (12 oz) celery, sliced
350 g (12 oz) leeks, sliced
2 garlic cloves, crushed
2 tablespoons light soy sauce
850 ml (1½ pints) vegetable stock
1 teaspoon caraway seeds
salt and freshly ground black pepper

1 Place the celery, leeks and garlic in a large saucepan and stir in the soy sauce. Pour over the vegetable stock, sprinkle in the caraway seeds and bring to the boil.

2 Reduce the heat, season to taste and simmer for 20 minutes.

3 Remove about a third of the soup and set aside. Liquidise the remainder using a blender or hand held blender, until smooth.

4 Return the blended and unblended soup to a clean saucepan. Heat through and then serve in warmed bowls.

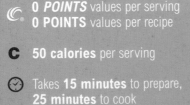

0 _POINTS_ values per serving
0 POINTS values per recipe

C   **50 calories** per serving

🕐   Takes **15 minutes** to prepare,
25 minutes to cook

V

✳   recommended

Italian-inspired Soup

This zero **POINTS** value soup makes a delicious meal.

Serves 12

1 head chicory
2 garlic cloves, crushed
160 g (5¾ oz) onions, chopped
40 g (1½ oz) spinach, chopped
2 courgettes, cubed
1 red pepper, de-seeded and
  chopped
¼ teaspoon crushed red pepper
  flakes
1 fennel bulb, thinly sliced

1.5 litres (2¾ pints) hot vegetable
  stock
2 x 400 g cans chopped tomatoes
2 sprigs fresh thyme, chopped
  finely
1 teaspoon fresh oregano,
  chopped finely
1 tablespoon fresh parsley,
  chopped
1 tablespoon fresh basil, chopped
salt and freshly ground black
  pepper

1 Place all the ingredients except the parsley, basil and seasoning in a
  large, lidded saucepan.

2 Cover the pan and bring to a boil over high heat. Reduce the heat to
  low and simmer, partly covered, for about 10 minutes.

3 Add the parsley and basil and season to taste. Stir well and serve in
  warmed bowls.

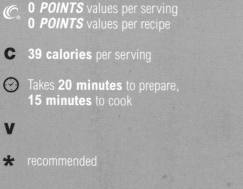

0 POINTS values per serving
0 POINTS values per recipe

C **39 calories** per serving

Takes **20 minutes** to prepare,
15 minutes to cook

V

* recommended

Fennel and Ginger Soup

This light soup makes the most of delicate fennel. It tastes delicious with its fiery hint of ginger and lemony zing.

Serves 4

low fat cooking spray
350 g (12 oz) fennel, chopped
5 shallots, chopped finely
1 garlic clove, crushed
2.5 cm (1 inch) fresh root ginger, peeled and chopped finely
a handful of fresh coriander, including stalks, chopped roughly
900 ml (1¾ pints) vegetable stock
finely grated zest of a lemon
salt and freshly ground black pepper

0 POINTS values per serving
0 POINTS values per recipe

C 28 calories per serving

Takes **10 minutes** to prepare, **25 minutes** to cook

V

* recommended

1 Heat a large, lidded, non stick saucepan and spray with the cooking spray. Sauté the fennel, shallots and garlic until softened, but not browned, about 3–4 minutes, adding a little water if necessary to prevent them from sticking.

2 Add the ginger, coriander, stock and lemon zest. Heat until almost boiling. Reduce the heat and simmer, covered, for 20 minutes.

3 Liquidise the soup in batches using a blender or hand held blender and return to the pan to warm through.

4 Season, ladle into warmed bowls and serve at once.

Tip If you wish, garnish each portion with a few fronds of feathery fennel, some coriander sprigs and 1 tablespoon of low fat natural yogurt, for an extra ½ **POINTS** value per serving.

Lunchtime Soups

These soups are all quick to make – ready to eat in less than 45 minutes and most ready in under 30 minutes – perfect for lunchtime. Try a chunky soup such as Haddock and Corn Chowder or Minestrone, or whizz up a creamy smooth lunchtime filler such as Carrot, Tarragon and Yogurt or Quick Tomato.

Fast and easy – soup is a great filler at lunchtime

Chunky Potato Soup

This soup is quick and easy to make using only a few inexpensive ingredients yet is delicious and nourishing. You could use any herb, fresh or dried, but we've chosen thyme as it goes especially well with potato.

Serves 4

low fat cooking spray
2 large onions, chopped finely
2 garlic cloves, crushed
1 kg (2 lb 4 oz) potatoes, peeled and diced into 2.5 cm (1-inch) cubes
a small bunch of thyme, chopped, plus extra to garnish
700 ml (25 fl oz) vegetable or chicken stock
150 ml (¼ pint) skimmed milk
salt and freshly ground black pepper

1 Heat a large, non stick saucepan and spray with the cooking spray. Stir fry the onions and garlic for 5 minutes until softened, adding a little water if necessary to prevent them from sticking.

2 Add the potatoes, seasoning, chopped thyme and stock, bring to the boil then simmer for 15 minutes until the potatoes are tender.

3 Remove from the heat and allow to cool a little then add the milk and stir through.

4 Check the seasoning and serve in warmed bowls. Garnish with sprigs of thyme.

3 *POINTS* values per serving
11½ **POINTS** values per recipe

C 225 calories per serving

Takes **5 minutes** to prepare, **20 minutes** to cook

V if using vegetable stock

✱ not recommended

Tip To make your own vegetable stock, reserve all the trimmings and peelings from various vegetables and then boil in a pan with 1.2 litres (2 pints) of water, a handful of peppercorns, ½ onion, a bay leaf and a bunch of herbs of your choice. Cook for 1 hour, then remove from the heat, allow to cool slightly and strain. It will keep in a jug in the refrigerator for a few days, or can be frozen for later use.

Chicken and Sweetcorn Soup

A super fast soup for a filling lunchtime meal.

Serves 4

850 ml (1½ pints) hot chicken stock
100 g (3½ oz) baby corn, sliced thinly
418 g can creamed sweetcorn
150 g (5½ oz) cooked skinless, boneless chicken breast, diced
1 tablespoon dry sherry
1 egg, beaten
2 spring onions, sliced finely, to garnish

1 Pour the stock into a large, lidded saucepan and bring to the boil. Add the sliced baby corn and cook for 5 minutes.

2 Add the creamed corn and diced chicken and simmer for a further 5 minutes.

3 Add the sherry, then pour in the beaten egg, stirring the soup so that the egg forms little threads.

4 Remove the pan from the heat, cover and leave to stand for 2 minutes.

5 Ladle into warmed bowls and scatter the spring onions on top.

2 *POINTS* values per serving
8 *POINTS* values per recipe

C 174 calories per serving

Takes **5 minutes** to prepare, **15 minutes** to cook

✳ not recommended

Italian Bean and Vegetable Soup

A chunky, hearty soup with a rustic touch, this will keep you feeling full for longer.

Serves 4

low fat cooking spray
1 onion, chopped finely
850 ml (1½ pints) hot vegetable stock
400 g can chopped tomatoes
200 g (7 oz) frozen mixed vegetables (e.g. peas, sweetcorn, carrots and green beans)
410 g can flageolet or borlotti beans, drained and rinsed
salt and freshly ground black pepper
2 tablespoons pesto sauce, to serve

---

2 *POINTS* values per serving
8 *POINTS* values per recipe

C 165 calories per serving

Takes **5 minutes** to prepare, **15 minutes** to cook

V

✱ recommended

1 Heat a large, lidded, non stick saucepan and spray with the cooking spray. Stir fry the onion over a high heat for 2–3 minutes, adding a little water if necessary to prevent it from sticking.

2 Add 4 tablespoons of the stock, cover the pan and cook for 3 minutes until the onion is softened.

3 Mix in the tomatoes, vegetables, beans and remaining stock.

4 Season, cover and simmer for 5 minutes or until the vegetables are tender.

5 Ladle into warmed bowls and top each bowlful with ½ tablespoon of pesto sauce to stir in as you eat.

Thai Shellfish Broth

Look out for packets of mixed seafood cocktail containing mussels, squid rings, crab sticks, prawns and scallops; they're perfect for this recipe.

Serves 4

low fat cooking spray
4 shallots, chopped
1 garlic clove, crushed
1 red chilli, de-seeded and sliced thinly
2.5 cm (1 inch) fresh root ginger, peeled and grated
2 stalks of lemon grass, trimmed and sliced very thinly
4 kaffir lime leaves (optional)
2 tablespoons fish sauce
1.2 litres (2 pints) fish stock
350 g (12 oz) seafood selection, such as prawns, mussels, scallops and squid
175 g (6 oz) cherry tomatoes, halved
50 g (1¾ oz) dried rice noodles
3 tablespoons chopped fresh coriander

1 Heat a large, non stick saucepan and spray with the cooking spray. Add the shallots, garlic and chilli.

2 Cook over a low heat for 2–3 minutes until just softened but not browned, adding a little water if necessary to prevent them from sticking.

3 Add the ginger, lemon grass, lime leaves, if using, fish sauce and stock and bring to the boil. Reduce the heat and simmer for 10 minutes.

4 Add the shellfish, tomatoes and noodles to the saucepan and cook for a further 5 minutes or until the noodles are tender.

5 Scatter the coriander over and ladle into deep warmed bowls to serve.

1½ *POINTS* values per serving
6½ POINTS values per recipe

C 159 calories per serving

Takes **10 minutes** to prepare, **20 minutes** to cook

✱ not recommended

Tips Look out for the small red Thai chillies for an authentic result. Take care though – they may be small but they're very fiery. Always wash your hands after cutting them up and never rub your eyes just after.

If you want to use kaffir lime leaves, look for them in the supermarket beside the herbs and spices where you'll find a dried version. You can also get them fresh in Asian supermarkets. They add a wonderfully refreshing flavour to Thai dishes.

Carrot, Tarragon and Yogurt Soup

This is a delicious, cheap soup that takes very little preparation and has a smooth creamy texture.

Serves 4

500 g (1 lb 2 oz) carrots, scrubbed and chopped

1.25 litres (2 pints) hot vegetable stock

1 onion, chopped

2 fresh tarragon sprigs

1 tablespoon lemon juice

salt and freshly ground black pepper

150 g (5 fl oz) 0% fat Greek yogurt, to serve

1 Put the carrots, stock, onion, 1 sprig of tarragon and seasoning into a large saucepan. Bring to the boil then simmer for 15 minutes until the vegetables are soft.

2 Strain the stock into a jug and reserve. Place the vegetables and cooked tarragon sprig in a blender, or use a hand held blender, and whizz until smooth.

3 Return the vegetable purée and stock to the pan and stir until well mixed, adding the lemon juice. Strip the leaves from the remaining tarragon sprig and stir into the soup.

4 Reheat gently if necessary and divide between four warmed bowls. Spoon the yogurt on top of the soup and serve.

½ *POINTS* values per serving
1 *POINTS* values per recipe

C **78 calories** per serving

Takes **5 minutes** to prepare, **20 minutes** to cook

V

* (before adding yogurt)

Asparagus and Fromage Frais Soup

½ POINTS VALUE

A silky, delicately flavoured spring soup.

Serves 4

low fat cooking spray
2 garlic cloves, sliced finely
1 large onion, chopped roughly
500 g (1 lb 2 oz) asparagus, woody stems cut
  off, chopped roughly
1.2 litres (2 pints) vegetable stock
100 g (3½ oz) virtually fat free fromage frais
salt and freshly ground black pepper
a small bunch of chervil, torn into pieces,
  to garnish (optional)

½ **POINTS** values per serving
2 **POINTS** values per recipe

C 65 calories per serving

Takes **5 minutes** to prepare,
15 minutes to cook

V

✱ recommended

1 Heat a large, non stick saucepan and spray with the cooking spray. Stir fry the garlic and onion for a few minutes, until softened and golden, adding a little water if necessary to prevent them from sticking.

2 Add the asparagus and stock and bring to the boil. Simmer for 5–10 minutes.

3 Liquidise the soup in batches using a blender or hand held blender and return to the pan to warm through.

4 Stir in the fromage frais and seasoning.

5 Serve in warmed bowls scattered with the chervil, if using.

Summer Pea, Ham and Mint Soup

A very quick, simple and fresh tasting soup that is perfect for a summer day.

Serves 2

low fat cooking spray
1 onion, sliced thinly
500 g (1 lb 2 oz) peas, freshly podded or frozen
600 ml (1 pint) vegetable stock
a bunch of fresh mint, chopped
100 g (3½ oz) lean ham, chopped into
  small pieces
salt and freshly ground black pepper

---

4 POINTS values per serving
8½ POINTS values per recipe

C **235 calories** per serving

Takes **5 minutes** to prepare,
15 minutes to cook

✱ not recommended

1 Heat a large, non stick saucepan and spray with the cooking spray. Stir fry the onion for 5 minutes until softened, adding a little water if necessary to prevent it from sticking.

2 Add the peas, stock, seasoning and half the mint. Bring to the boil and then simmer for 5 minutes.

3 Add the rest of the mint, but reserve a little for garnishing.

4 Liquidise the soup in batches using a blender or hand held blender and return to the pan.

5 Add the ham and warm through, check the seasoning and serve in warmed bowls garnished with the reserved mint and more black pepper.

Creamy Watercress Soup

This soup is delicious served chilled in the summer months. If you plan to do this, make it the day before, then refrigerate it overnight.

Serves 4

25 g (1 oz) low fat spread
1 large onion, chopped
2 bunches of watercress
a generous handful of parsley
600 ml (1 pint) hot vegetable stock
200 g (7 oz) low fat soft cheese
2 tablespoons cornflour
425 ml (¾ pint) skimmed milk
salt and freshly ground black pepper
4 tablespoons low fat natural yogurt, to serve

3 *POINTS* values per serving
12½ *POINTS* values per recipe

C   188 calories per serving

Takes **10 minutes** to prepare,
30 minutes to cook

V

✱   recommended

1 Melt the low fat spread in a large, lidded, non stick saucepan and fry the onion gently over a low heat for about 3 minutes, until softened but not browned, adding a little water if necessary to prevent it from sticking.

2 Reserve a few watercress sprigs for garnish, then add the remainder to the saucepan with all the parsley – including the stems (they will add to the finished flavour of the soup). You don't have to chop the watercress or parsley as it will be blended later.

3 Pour the stock into the saucepan and bring up to the boil, then cover and reduce the heat to low. Simmer gently for 15–20 minutes.

4 Liquidise the soup in batches using a blender or hand held blender. Add the low fat soft cheese and whizz until smooth. Return the soup to the saucepan.

5 Blend the cornflour with 3–4 tablespoons of the milk. Add to the soup with the remaining milk and bring up to the boil, stirring, until the soup thickens. Simmer gently for about 2 minutes.

6 Season the soup, ladle into warmed bowls and garnish each portion with a spoonful of yogurt and the remaining sprigs of watercress.

Variation You could use 350 g (12 oz) baby spinach leaves or rocket instead of watercress for a change, for the same *POINTS* values. Just make sure you wash the leaves thoroughly first.

Summer Vegetable Soup

Rather like a gazpacho, this is a raw, chilled soup packed with summer flavours – nutritional rocket fuel served with crunchy, garlicky croûtons.

Serves 2

400 g (14 oz) ripe tomatoes, chopped roughly

1 courgette, chopped roughly

½ cucumber, chopped

1 red onion, chopped roughly, with some diced finely for garnish

½ red pepper, chopped roughly, with some diced finely for garnish

1 teaspoon balsamic vinegar

300 ml (½ pint) passata

¼ teaspoon Tabasco sauce

1 tablespoon Worcestershire sauce

1 tablespoon soy sauce

a large bunch of basil, chopped roughly, but the small leaves kept whole for garnish

salt and freshly ground black pepper

For the croûtons

2 thick slices wholemeal bread, cubed

1 garlic clove, crushed

low fat cooking spray

1½ **POINTS** values per serving
3 **POINTS** values per recipe

C 245 calories per serving

Takes **25 minutes** + chilling

V if not using Worcestershire sauce

✱ recommended without the croûtons

1 For the croûtons, preheat the oven to Gas Mark 4/180°C/fan oven 160°C. On a baking tray, toss the bread cubes with the garlic and seasoning and then spray with the cooking spray. Bake for 15–20 minutes, shaking the tray occasionally and keeping a close eye on the croûtons, until they are golden brown and crisp.

2 Meanwhile, place all the soup ingredients, except those for the garnish, in a blender, or use a hand held blender, and blend until smooth, adding a little cold water if too thick.

3 Tip the soup into bowls (or chill in the fridge first) and serve scattered with the remaining finely diced red onion, red pepper, small basil leaves and the croûtons.

Creamy Garlic Mushroom Soup

A wonderful way to use up mushrooms, this is full of flavour and filling.

Serves 2

low fat cooking spray
1 onion, chopped roughly
2 plump garlic cloves, crushed
300 g (10½ oz) button or field mushrooms, cleaned and chopped roughly
500 ml (18 fl oz) skimmed milk
2 slices dried porcini mushrooms
2 x 400 g cans butter beans, drained and rinsed
1 teaspoon dried or fresh thyme, chopped
salt and freshly ground black pepper
a small bunch of fresh parsley or thyme, chopped finely, to serve

3 POINTS values per serving
6½ POINTS values per recipe

C **394 calories** per serving

Takes **10 minutes** to prepare,
15 minutes to cook

V

✱ recommended

1 Heat a large, non stick saucepan and spray with the cooking spray. Gently fry the onion and garlic for a minute, adding a little water if necessary to prevent them from sticking.

2 Add the button or field mushrooms and stir fry together for a few minutes on a high heat.

3 Once the mushrooms start to look cooked, add the milk, porcini mushrooms, beans and thyme.

4 Use a wooden spoon to scrape up any bits that have caught on the bottom of the pan into the soup.

5 Bring to the boil, then turn down to a simmer for 10 minutes.

6 Liquidise the soup in batches using a blender or hand held blender and return to the pan to warm through. Taste and adjust the seasoning if necessary.

7 Serve in warmed bowls, sprinkled with fresh parsley or thyme.

Garden Vegetable Soup

The perfect bowl of soup for spring.

Serves 4

low fat cooking spray
1 onion, finely chopped
350 g (12 oz) spinach or watercress
125 g (4½ oz) fresh or frozen peas
1 tablespoon chopped fresh mint
450 ml (16 fl oz) hot vegetable stock
200 g (7 oz) low fat soft cheese
2 tablespoons cornflour
450 ml (16 fl oz) skimmed milk
salt and freshly ground black pepper
mint sprigs, to garnish

2½ *POINTS* values per serving
10 *POINTS* values per recipe

C 198 calories per serving

Takes **10 minutes** to prepare,
25 minutes to cook

V

✳ recommended

1 Spray a large, non stick saucepan with the cooking spray and cook the onion until softened, adding a little water if necessary to prevent it from sticking.

2 Add the spinach or watercress and cook until wilted, for about 3–4 minutes.

3 Add most of the peas, reserving some for later, along with the chopped mint and stock. Bring up to the boil, then reduce the heat and simmer for 10 minutes.

4 Transfer to a blender or use a hand held blender. Add most of the soft cheese, reserving some for garnishing, and liquidise until smooth. Return to the saucepan.

5 Blend the cornflour with 2–3 tablespoons of the milk, then add to the saucepan with the remaining milk and reserved peas.

6 Bring to the boil, stirring until thickened, then cook gently for 2 minutes.

7 Season to taste, then serve in warmed bowls, topped with the reserved soft cheese and mint sprigs.

Sweetcorn Soup

This couldn't be easier – using creamed sweetcorn saves time and it tastes delicious.

Serves 6

1.2 litres (2 pints) vegetable stock
418 g can creamed sweetcorn
2 tablespoons cornflour
30 ml (1 fl oz) dry sherry
4 spring onions, chopped finely
2 eggs, beaten

1½ *POINTS* values per serving
9½ *POINTS* values per recipe

C 100 calories per serving

Takes **10 minutes**

V

* recommended after step 3

1 Bring the stock to the boil in a large saucepan and stir in the creamed sweetcorn.

2 Blend the cornflour with 2 tablespoons of cold water. Add the cornflour paste to the stock, stir until thickened and then simmer gently for 2 minutes.

3 Add the sherry and half the spring onions.

4 Take the soup off the boil and slowly pour the beaten eggs into the soup in a thin stream, stirring gently. They will cook as you pour them in and look like thin white ribbons.

5 Transfer the soup to warmed bowls and serve, topped with the remaining spring onions.

Chicken Noodle Soup

This broth is well known for its comforting qualities. It's also a great way to use up leftover chicken.

Serves 4

low fat cooking spray
2 onions, sliced thinly
2 garlic cloves, crushed
150 g (5½ oz) cooked, skinless, boneless chicken breast, shredded
2 litres (3½ pints) chicken stock
300 g (10½ oz) spaghetti, broken up, or spaghettini
salt and freshly ground black pepper

1 Heat a large, lidded, non stick saucepan over a high heat, spray with the cooking spray, then stir fry the onions and garlic for 2 minutes, adding a little water if necessary to prevent them from sticking.

2 Turn down the heat, cover and leave the onions and garlic to sweat for 10 minutes.

3 Add the chicken and stock and bring to the boil.

4 Add the pasta and simmer for 10 minutes.

5 Check the seasoning and serve in warmed bowls.

4½ **POINTS** values per serving
18 POINTS values per recipe

C **355 calories** per serving

Takes **5 minutes** to prepare,
25 minutes to cook

* not recommended

Minestrone Soup

A colourful, fun soup that is great for an easy lunch with friends.

Serves 4

low fat cooking spray
1 large onion, chopped
2 garlic cloves, crushed
3 carrots, peeled and sliced thinly
100 g (3½ oz) whole green beans, cut in half crossways
300 g (10½ oz) canned mixed pulses, drained

400 g can chopped tomatoes
2 teaspoons dried basil
1 litre (1¾ pints) vegetable stock
30 g (1¼ oz) soup pasta or macaroni
salt and freshly ground black pepper

1 Heat a large, lidded, non stick saucepan to a medium heat, spray with the cooking spray and stir fry the onion and garlic for 3 minutes, adding a little water if necessary to prevent them from sticking.

2 Add the carrots, beans, pulses, tomatoes, basil and stock and bring to the boil. Cover and simmer for 15 minutes or until the carrots are just tender.

3 Add the pasta and cook for a further 10 minutes or until the pasta is cooked.

4 Adjust the seasoning and serve immediately in warmed bowls or mugs.

1½ *POINTS* values per serving
6½ *POINTS* values per recipe

C **153 calories** per serving

Takes **5 minutes** to prepare, **30 minutes** to cook

V

✱ recommended

Jaipur-style Dahl Soup

Dahl is an Indian lentil dish that has many different regional versions. This soup keeps very well, covered, in the fridge, for up to 3 days. Serve with 1 tablespoon of low fat natural yogurt per person, for an extra ½ **POINTS** value per serving.

Serves 4

low fat cooking spray
3 garlic cloves, sliced finely
2 tablespoons cumin seeds
½ teaspoon fennel seeds
2.5 cm (1 inch) fresh root ginger, peeled and chopped
1–2 green chillies, de-seeded and chopped finely (optional)
1.2 litres (2 pints) vegetable stock
½ teaspoon ground turmeric
200 g (7 oz) red lentils, drained and rinsed
2 carrots, peeled and diced finely
½ cauliflower, cut into small florets
juice of half a lemon
a small bunch of fresh coriander, chopped
salt and freshly ground black pepper

½ **POINTS** values per serving
3 **POINTS** values per recipe

C 215 **calories** per serving

Takes **5 minutes** to prepare,
25 minutes to cook

V

✳ recommended

1 Heat a large, lidded, non stick saucepan and spray with the cooking spray. Stir fry the garlic until golden, adding a little water if necessary to prevent it from sticking.

2 Add the cumin, fennel, ginger and chillies, if using, and stir fry for a further few minutes until they become fragrant.

3 Add the stock, turmeric and lentils and stir together.

4 Bring to the boil, removing any froth that collects on the top, and then add the vegetables.

5 Cover and simmer for 15 minutes and then add the lemon juice and coriander.

6 Check the seasoning and serve in warmed bowls.

Chunky Chicken and Vegetable Soup

This is a delicious and filling main meal soup. Make lots and then freeze what you don't eat for a quick snack when you are feeling hungry.

Serves 4

1.5 litres (2¾ pints) chicken stock
2 x 100 g (3½ oz) skinless, boneless chicken breasts
1 leek, sliced thinly
1 carrot, peeled and grated coarsely
a good pinch of dried mixed herbs or dried thyme
2 tablespoons quick cook macaroni or small soup pasta shapes
1 small courgette, chopped
3 tablespoons garden peas
1 sprig of fresh basil, torn (optional)
salt and freshly ground black pepper

1 Pour the chicken stock into a large saucepan and bring to the boil.

2 Carefully add the chicken breasts, leek, carrot, dried herbs and seasoning. Simmer for 15 minutes until the chicken is cooked. Remove the chicken with a slotted spoon.

3 Stir the pasta, courgette and peas into the pan. Simmer for a further 5 minutes.

4 Meanwhile, cut the chicken into small cubes.

5 Return the chicken to the soup and check the seasoning.

6 Stir in the basil, if using, and serve the soup in warmed bowls.

1½ **POINTS** values per serving
5 **POINTS** values per recipe

C 130 **calories** per serving

Takes **10 minutes** to prepare, **20 minutes** to cook

✱ recommended

Carrot and Orange Soup

The combination of fresh carrots and tangy orange juice makes this a really refreshing soup.

Serves 4

low fat cooking spray
1 large onion, chopped
700 g (1 lb 9 oz) carrots, peeled and grated
300 g (10½ oz) potatoes, peeled and grated

grated zest and juice of an orange
600 ml (1 pint) boiling water
salt and freshly ground black pepper
a handful of fresh parsley or coriander, chopped, to serve

1 Heat a large, lidded, non stick saucepan and spray with the cooking spray. Stir fry the onion for 3–4 minutes, adding a little water if necessary to prevent it from sticking.

2 Add the carrots, potatoes and seasoning. Stir the vegetables thoroughly and then cover the pan. Leave on a low heat for 5 minutes to allow the vegetables to sweat.

3 Add the orange zest and then cover the vegetables with the boiling water. Cover the pan again and simmer for 15–20 minutes.

4 Add the orange juice and liquidise the soup in batches using a blender or hand held blender. Return to the pan to warm through, check the seasoning and serve garnished with the orange segments and freshly chopped parsley or coriander.

1 *POINTS* values per serving
4 *POINTS* values per recipe

C 131 **calories** per serving

Takes **10 minutes** to prepare, **35 minutes** to cook

V

* recommended

Rosemary and Bean Soup

A warming autumnal soup with an unusual flavour that is sure to please.

Serves 4

low fat cooking spray
4 garlic cloves, left in skins
4 x 400 g cans cannellini or borlotti or butter
  beans, drained and rinsed
1 onion, chopped into wedges
1 lemon, cut into quarters
2 sprigs rosemary, stems removed, plus
  extra for garnish
1 teaspoon dried oregano
1 litre (1¾ pints) vegetable stock
4 tablespoons low fat natural yogurt
salt and freshly ground black pepper

---

3 **POINTS** values per serving
11½ **POINTS** values per recipe

C **291 calories** per serving

Takes **10 minutes** to prepare,
30 minutes to cook

V

* recommended

1 Preheat the oven to Gas Mark 6/200°C/fan oven 180°C. Spray a large, non stick roasting tin with the cooking spray.

2 Add the garlic cloves, beans, onion, lemon, rosemary sprigs and oregano to the tin and spray again with the cooking spray. Toss together and roast for 20 minutes, or until golden.

3 Remove from the oven and squash the lemon pieces and garlic cloves with a fork. Discard the lemon rind and garlic skins, then add the stock to the roasting tin.

4 Scrape up any juices with a wooden spatula and carefully tip the hot beans and stock into a saucepan or blender.

5 Liquidise the soup in batches using a blender or hand held blender to make a thick soup.

6 Return to the pan to warm through and season to taste.

7 Serve garnished with chopped rosemary, a tablespoon of low fat natural yogurt per serving and freshly ground black pepper.

Tomato and Rice Soup

This soup is very quick to make and satisfying to eat. Serve with a medium crusty roll per person, for an extra 2 **POINTS** values per serving.

Serves 4

low fat cooking spray
1 large onion, chopped
2 garlic cloves, crushed
2 x 400 g cans chopped tomatoes
1 tablespoon clear honey
1.2 litres (2 pints) vegetable stock
leaves from a small bunch of parsley, thyme, rosemary or basil, chopped
100 g (3½ oz) basmati rice
salt and freshly ground black pepper

1 Heat a large, non stick saucepan and spray with the cooking spray. Stir fry the onion and garlic for 5 minutes until softened, adding a little water if necessary to prevent them from sticking.

2 Add the tomatoes, seasoning and honey, bring to the boil and simmer for 10 minutes.

3 Add the stock, herbs and rice and simmer a further 25 minutes.

4 Serve in warmed bowls.

1½ **POINTS** values per serving
6 POINTS values per recipe

C 155 calories per serving

Takes **5 minutes** to prepare, **40 minutes** to cook

V

✱ not recommended

Variation Use 3 teaspoons of caster sugar instead of the honey, for the same **POINTS** values.

Haddock and Corn Chowder

Serve this with two cream crackers per serving, adding 1 **POINTS** value per portion.

Serves 4

200 g (7 oz) potatoes, peeled and chopped finely

4 spring onions, chopped

2 teaspoons low fat spread

½ teaspoon mild curry powder (optional)

300 ml (½ pint) skimmed milk

300 ml (½ pint) fish, vegetable or chicken stock

300 g (10½ oz) smoked haddock, prepared and cut into small cubes (see Tip)

198 g can sweetcorn, drained and the liquid reserved

salt and freshly ground black pepper

1 tablespoon chopped fresh parsley, to garnish

1 Put the potatoes, spring onions, low fat spread and curry powder, if using, into a large, lidded, non stick saucepan with 4 tablespoons of water. Heat until the mixture is sizzling, and then cover and simmer for 10 minutes, shaking occasionally. Do not let the ingredients burn.

2 Remove the cover, stir in the milk and stock, and bring to the boil. Reduce the heat and simmer for 5 minutes.

3 Add the fish along with the sweetcorn and reserved liquid. Gently boil and cook for 5 more minutes. Check the seasoning and serve, sprinkled with the parsley, in warmed bowls.

2½ **POINTS** values per serving
9½ **POINTS** values per recipe

C 175 calories per serving

Takes **10 minutes** to prepare, **20 minutes** to cook

* recommended

Tips Curry powder has zero **POINTS** values, so it's always best to use it rather than curry pastes, which have a high oil content.

To skin the fish, slide a sharp, straight bladed knife between the flesh and the skin of the fish, and work in a sawing motion to remove all the skin. With your fingertips, check the flesh for any pin bones and pull them out.

Fresh Herb Soup

This soup is perfect for using up a glut of garden fresh herbs. It is delicious when served chilled in the summer. Ladle it into chilled bowls and add an ice cube to each portion.

Serves 4

15 g (½ oz) low fat spread
1 bunch spring onions, trimmed and chopped
225 g (8 oz) spinach, thoroughly washed
4 tablespoons mixed chopped fresh herbs
 (e.g. chives, parsley, marjoram, basil)
300 ml (½ pint) vegetable stock
1 tablespoon green pesto sauce
200 g (7 oz) low fat soft cheese
1 tablespoon cornflour
425 ml (¾ pint) skimmed milk
salt and freshly ground black pepper

To serve
4 tablespoons low fat natural yogurt
fresh herb sprigs, optional

1 Melt the low fat spread in a large, lidded, non stick saucepan and sauté the spring onions until softened, about 3–5 minutes, adding a little water if necessary to prevent them from sticking.

2 Add the spinach and cook, stirring occasionally, until it has wilted, about another 2 minutes.

3 Add the herbs and vegetable stock to the saucepan and bring to the boil, then add the pesto sauce. Reduce the heat, cover and simmer for 10 minutes.

4 Transfer the soup to a blender, or use a hand held blender, and add the soft cheese. Whizz for about 15–20 seconds until smooth, then return to the saucepan.

5 Blend the cornflour with 2–3 tablespoons of the milk, add to the soup with the remaining milk and bring up to the boil, stirring constantly until thickened and smooth.

6 Season to taste, then serve in warmed bowls, topped with yogurt and garnished with sprigs of fresh herbs, if desired.

2½ *POINTS* values per serving
10½ **POINTS** values per recipe

C 174 **calories** per serving

Takes **10 minutes** to prepare,
25 minutes to cook

V

✳ recommended

Quick Tomato Soup

Serves 4

1 large onion, chopped
2 celery sticks, chopped
2 garlic cloves, crushed
450 ml (16 fl oz) hot vegetable
  stock
2 x 400 g cans chopped tomatoes
2 tablespoons tomato purée
1 tablespoon dried mixed herbs

1 teaspoon dark or light
  muscovado sugar
1 tablespoon cornflour
salt and freshly ground black
  pepper

To serve
4 tablespoons low fat natural
  yogurt
celery leaves (optional)

1 Put the onion, celery and garlic in a large saucepan and pour in the
  stock. Bring to the boil, then reduce the heat. Simmer for 5 minutes.
  Add the chopped tomatoes, tomato purée, dried herbs and muscovado
  sugar. Bring to the boil and reduce the heat. Simmer for 5 minutes.

2 Liquidise the soup in batches using a blender or hand held blender
  and return to the pan. Blend the cornflour with 3 tablespoons of cold
  water and stir in.

3 Reheat gently, stirring until the soup thickens. Cook for another
  minute or two. Season to taste. Serve in warmed bowls topped with
  a tablespoon of low fat natural yogurt, a few celery leaves, if using,
  and a little more ground black pepper.

1 POINTS values per serving
3 POINTS values per recipe

C 90 calories per serving

Takes **10 minutes** to prepare,
15 minutes to cook

V

✻ recommended

Tip Try using canned whole plum tomatoes in this recipe – chop them
roughly first. This only takes a few moments and it makes the recipe
more economical.

Variation To make a cream of tomato soup, add a 200 g tub of low fat
soft cheese when whizzing, for an extra 1½ **POINTS** values per serving.

Hearty and Filling Soups

These soups are meals in themselves. Full of flavour and filling ingredients, they are suitable for a hearty lunch or a light supper. Try the unusual, such as Chicken Noodle Soup with Coconut Milk or Moroccan Chicken. Or variations on an old favourite, such as Fisherman's Catch and Main Meal Minestrone.

Guaranteed to help fill you up just when you need it

Main Meal Minestrone

(3 POINTS VALUE)

Almost a mini casserole, this delicious soup will warm the cockles of your heart.

Serves 4

225 g (8 oz) extra lean beef mince
1 teaspoon paprika
175 g (6 oz) carrots, peeled and diced
1 red pepper, de-seeded and chopped
1 onion, chopped
1 garlic clove, crushed
225 g (8 oz) courgettes, chopped
400 g can chopped tomatoes
850 ml (1½ pints) beef stock
100 g (3½ oz) soup pasta or quick cook
  macaroni
2 tablespoons chopped fresh flat leaf parsley
salt and freshly ground black pepper

3 **POINTS** values per serving
13 **POINTS** values per recipe

C 275 **calories** per serving

Takes **15 minutes** to prepare,
30 minutes to cook

✱ recommended

1 Heat a large, lidded, non stick saucepan, add the mince and dry fry until evenly browned.

2 Stir in the paprika, carrots, red pepper, onion, garlic and courgettes and cook for 2 minutes.

3 Stir in the tomatoes and stock, and bring to the boil. Reduce the heat, cover and simmer for 15 minutes.

4 Add the pasta and season to taste. Cook for a further 10 minutes or until the pasta is tender.

5 Stir in the parsley and serve the soup in warmed bowls.

Variation Use turkey or pork mince as an alternative to beef, but remember to change the type of stock you use, too. The **POINTS** values per serving will be 2½ and 3 respectively.

Pasta, Pork and Bean Soup

This is a lovely, thick, comforting soup. The earthy flavour of rosemary perfectly complements the beans and pork. Any cut of pork will do as long as it is off the bone and lean.

Serves 4

low fat cooking spray
250 g (9 oz) cubed pork
1 red onion, diced
2 garlic cloves, crushed
2 teaspoons dried rosemary or 2 tablespoons chopped fresh rosemary
2 litres (3½ pints) chicken stock
400 g can red kidney beans
200 g (7 oz) pasta
salt and freshly ground black pepper

4½ **POINTS** values per serving
17½ **POINTS** values per recipe

C 345 **calories** per serving

Takes **10 minutes** to prepare,
10 minutes to cook

✱ recommended

1 Heat a large, non stick saucepan and spray with the cooking spray. Fry the pork over a high heat for 5 minutes or until golden brown.

2 Add the onion, garlic, rosemary and seasoning and stir fry until softened – about 4 minutes, adding a little water if necessary to prevent them from sticking.

3 Add the stock and bring to the boil.

4 Add the beans and pasta and simmer for 10 minutes for small pasta or 15 minutes for larger pasta.

5 Liquidise the soup in batches using a blender or hand held blender and return to the pan to warm through. Check the seasoning before serving in warmed bowls.

Tip You can use 50 g (1¾ oz) dried beans. Soak them in plenty of water overnight. Cook them, again in plenty of water, without seasoning, for 45 minutes after they have come to the boil.

Cauliflower and Stilton Soup

3½ POINTS VALUE

Low fat soft cheese gives a delightfully creamy texture to this unusual soup.

Serves 4

15 g (½ oz) low fat spread
1 onion, chopped
2 garlic cloves, crushed
½ small cauliflower, broken into florets
850 ml (1½ pints) hot vegetable stock
300 ml (½ pint) skimmed milk
200 g (7 oz) low fat soft cheese
2 tablespoons chopped fresh chives
50 g (1¾ oz) blue Stilton cheese, crumbled
salt and freshly ground black pepper

3½ **POINTS** values per serving
13½ **POINTS** values per recipe

C 186 **calories** per serving

Takes **10 minutes** to prepare,
35 minutes to cook

V

✱ recommended

1 Melt the low fat spread in a large, lidded, non stick saucepan and sauté the onion and garlic for about 5 minutes, until softened, adding a little water if necessary to prevent them from sticking.

2 Add the cauliflower and vegetable stock to the saucepan and bring up to the boil.

3 Cover and cook over a very low heat for about 20 minutes, until the cauliflower is tender.

4 Transfer to a blender, or use a hand held blender, add the milk, and whizz for about 15 seconds.

5 Reserving 2 tablespoons of low fat soft cheese, add the remainder to the soup with half the chives. Whizz for a few more seconds until smooth.

6 Return to the saucepan, add the Stilton cheese, then reheat gently. Season to taste.

7 Ladle the soup into warmed bowls and spoon half a tablespoon of soft cheese on top of each portion. Sprinkle with the remaining chives and a little extra ground black pepper and serve at once.

Variation Use grated Cheddar cheese if you're not keen on blue cheese – a mature one will give the best flavour. The **POINTS** values per serving will remain the same.

Moroccan Chicken Soup

A cross between a soup and a stew, this Moroccan delight will satisfy all of your senses. If you want the soup to taste really authentic, add a dash of fiery Tabasco sauce before serving.

Serves 4

low fat cooking spray
1 onion, chopped finely
2 garlic cloves, crushed
1 green chilli, de-seeded and diced
225 g (8 oz) chicken mince
1 teaspoon ground cinnamon
1 teaspoon ground cumin
½ teaspoon ground coriander
1.2 litres (2 pints) chicken stock
410 g can chick peas, drained and rinsed
3 tablespoons tomato purée
50 g (1¾ oz) dry couscous
3 tablespoons fresh chopped mint
juice of a lemon

3½ **POINTS** values per serving
14½ **POINTS** values per recipe

C 225 **calories** per serving

Takes **10 minutes** to prepare,
35 minutes to cook

* recommended before adding the couscous

1 Heat a large, lidded, non stick saucepan and spray with the cooking spray. Add the onion and brown for 5 minutes, adding a little water if necessary to prevent it from sticking.

2 Add the garlic, chilli and chicken mince and cook, stirring to break up the mince, until lightly coloured.

3 Mix in the ground spices and cook for 30 seconds before adding the chicken stock, chick peas and tomato purée.

4 Bring to the boil, cover and simmer for 20 minutes.

5 Remove from the heat and stir in the couscous, mint and lemon juice.

6 Cover the pan and leave to stand for 5 minutes until the couscous is tender.

7 Ladle into warmed bowls to serve.

Variation For a vegetarian version of this soup, replace the chicken mince with minced Quorn and use vegetable stock instead of chicken stock. The **POINTS** values will remain the same.

Soupe Au Pistou

This soup is full of delicious and nutritious vegetables, beans and pasta and the addition of pistou, which is like pesto but without the pine kernels, gives it a wonderfully aromatic flavour.

Serves 4

low fat cooking spray
1 onion, chopped
2 leeks, chopped finely
400 g can chopped tomatoes
2 small potatoes, diced finely
350 g (12 oz) courgettes, diced finely
2 carrots, peeled and diced finely
300 g can haricot beans, drained
100 g (3½ oz) green beans, cut into quarters
50 g (1¾ oz) spaghettini, broken into short pieces
a bunch of flat leaf parsley, chopped
salt and freshly ground black pepper

For the pistou

a bunch of basil
1 garlic clove, crushed
2 tablespoons olive oil
25 g (1 oz) Parmesan cheese, freshly grated
1 tablespoon low fat soft cheese

---

4 POINTS values per serving
16 POINTS values per recipe

C **320 calories** per serving

Takes **25 minutes** to prepare + soaking overnight, **50 minutes** to cook

V

✱ not recommended

1 Heat a large, lidded, non stick saucepan and spray with the cooking spray. Sauté the onion and leeks, adding a little water if necessary to prevent them from sticking.

2 After 2 minutes, add the tomatoes, potatoes, courgettes, carrots, haricot beans and green beans.

3 Mix everything together and then pour over 2 litres (3½ pints) hot water. Cover and simmer for 30 minutes.

4 Meanwhile, make the pistou by placing the basil, garlic and oil in a blender, or use a hand held blender. Whizz until smooth. If the mixture is too dry, add a little water. Scrape down the jug and then add the cheeses. Pulse quickly until mixed in.

5 Add the pasta and parsley to the soup, season and cook for a further 10 minutes.

6 Just before serving, stir in the pistou, saving a little to blob on top.

Lentil, Porcini and Bacon Soup

Porcini is the Italian word for cep mushrooms usually sold sliced and dried. Any dried mushrooms will do as they impart a lovely strong, earthy flavour to this thick and comforting soup.

Serves 4

low fat cooking spray
1 large onion, chopped finely
200 g (7 oz) thickly sliced lean back bacon, all fat removed, sliced into small pieces
2 celery sticks, chopped finely
200 g (7 oz) dried red or brown lentils
1.2 litres (2 pints) vegetable stock
15 g (½ oz) porcini, chopped finely
a small bunch of fresh thyme or tarragon, tough stems removed, chopped (optional)
salt and freshly ground black pepper

5 POINTS values per serving
21 POINTS values per recipe

C 255 calories per serving

Takes **5 minutes** to prepare, **30 minutes** to cook

✱ recommended

1 Heat a large, non stick saucepan and spray with the cooking spray. Stir fry the onion with the bacon and celery until golden and softened, adding a little water if necessary to prevent them from sticking.

2 Add the lentils, stock, porcini and thyme or tarragon, if using, reserving a few sprigs, and bring to the boil.

3 Turn down the heat and simmer for 20 minutes, until the lentils are tender.

4 Check the seasoning and serve the soup in warmed bowls, garnished with the reserved tarragon or thyme, if using.

Chunky Chicken Chowder

This soup is ideal for preparing in advance.

Serves 2

165 g (5¾ oz) skinless boneless chicken
   breast, diced
425 ml (¾ pint) chicken or vegetable stock
2 carrots, peeled and grated
2 leeks, sliced
½ swede, peeled and diced
2 tablespoons dried yellow lentils, rinsed
300 ml (½ pint) semi skimmed milk
2 tablespoons fresh, frozen or canned sweetcorn
salt and freshly ground black pepper

3½ **POINTS** values per serving
7 **POINTS** values per recipe

C 330 **calories** per serving

Takes **15 minutes** to prepare,
40 minutes to cook

✱ recommended

1 Place all the ingredients except the milk, sweetcorn and seasoning in a large saucepan and bring to the boil.

2 Turn down the heat and simmer for 25–30 minutes.

3 Add the milk and sweetcorn.

4 Season and warm through for a further 10 minutes on a gentle heat before serving in warmed bowls.

Spicy Beef and Noodle Soup

A tangy and slightly hot Oriental soup with strips of beef and noodles.

Serves 2

low fat cooking spray

300 g (10½ oz) lean rump beef, cut into thin strips

1 litre (1¾ pints) beef stock

2 lemongrass sticks, tough outer leaves removed, chopped

2 red chillies, de-seeded and diced

juice of 2 limes

125 g (4½ oz) dried thread egg noodles

75 g (2¾ oz) mange tout

110 g (4 oz) baby corn

coriander leaves, to garnish

6½ **POINTS** values per serving
13 **POINTS** values per recipe

C 311 **calories** per serving

Takes **10 minutes** to prepare, **20 minutes** to cook

✱ not recommended

1 Heat a large, lidded, non stick saucepan and spray with the cooking spray. Add the beef and stir fry for 3–5 minutes until browned all over.

2 Add the stock, lemongrass, chillies and lime juice.

3 Bring to the boil, cover and simmer for 10 minutes until the beef is tender.

4 Add the noodles, mange tout and baby corn. Bring to the boil. Simmer gently for 5 minutes until the noodles are cooked and the vegetables tender.

5 Garnish with the coriander before serving in warmed bowls.

Tip Try this recipe with the equivalent weight in skinless boneless chicken breast, for a **POINTS** value of 5½ per serving.

Quick Mussel Soup

A quick, warming and delicious soup – great for the cold winter months.

Serves 4

low fat cooking spray
1 onion, chopped finely
1 celery stick, chopped finely
1 carrot, peeled and chopped finely
300 g (10½ oz) sweet potatoes or potatoes,
    diced into 1 cm (½ inch) cubes
1.2 litres (2 pints) vegetable stock
2 x 400 g cans chopped tomatoes
450 g (1 lb) canned mussels
200 g (7 oz) green beans, chopped
a small bunch of soft thyme, chopped
salt and freshly ground black pepper

3 **POINTS** values per serving
12½ **POINTS** values per recipe

C 263 **calories** per serving

Takes **20 minutes** to prepare,
20 minutes to cook

✱ not recommended

1 Heat a large, non stick saucepan and spray with the cooking spray. Stir fry the onion, celery, carrot and potatoes for a few minutes, adding a little water if necessary to prevent them from sticking.

2 Add the stock and bring to the boil. Simmer for 10 minutes, then add the tomatoes.

3 Simmer for a further 10 minutes.

4 Finally, add the mussels, beans and thyme. Simmer gently for 2 minutes.

5 Season to taste, check that the potatoes are tender, then serve in warmed bowls.

Yellow Split Pea Soup

Yellow split peas make this a filling and substantial soup that is ideal for the colder months.

Serves 4

225 g (8 oz) dried yellow split peas
½ teaspoon salt
25 g (1 oz) low fat spread
1 large onion, chopped
2 carrots, peeled and chopped finely
1 litre (1¾ pints) hot ham or vegetable stock
1 teaspoon dried thyme
salt and freshly ground black pepper
1 tablespoon chopped fresh parsley, to garnish

3 POINTS values per serving
12 POINTS values per recipe

C **245 calories** per serving

Takes **10 minutes** to prepare + soaking,
1–1½ hours to cook

V if using vegetable stock

* recommended

1 Put the split peas into a bowl and cover with boiling water. Add ½ teaspoon of salt, then leave to soak for about 12 hours, or overnight. Rinse and drain well.

2 Melt the low fat spread in a large, lidded, non stick saucepan and add the onion. Sauté for about 5 minutes over a medium heat, until lightly browned, adding a little water if necessary to prevent it from sticking.

3 Add the carrots to the saucepan and stir well.

4 Pour the stock into the saucepan and add the dried thyme and soaked split peas. Bring up to the boil, then reduce the heat, cover and simmer until the split peas are tender, about 1–1½ hours.

5 Season to taste and serve in warmed bowls, garnished with chopped fresh parsley.

Variations For a quicker cooking time with less preparation, use red lentils instead of split peas. They don't need to be pre-soaked, and they only take about 45 minutes to cook. The **POINTS** values will remain the same.

Mexican Ham and Bean Soup

A hearty, spicy soup, which can be spiced up more if you wish – just add more chilli powder and you could be on your way to Mexico.

Serves 4

low fat cooking spray
1 onion, chopped
200 g (7 oz) ham, cut into short strips
50 g (1¾ oz) dried split red lentils
400 g can flageolet beans, drained and rinsed
410 g can cannellini beans, drained and rinsed
1–2 teaspoons chilli powder
1.2 litres (2 pints) vegetable stock
1 tablespoon tomato purée
salt and freshly ground black pepper
1 tablespoon chopped fresh parsley, to serve

4½ **POINTS** values per serving
18 **POINTS** values per recipe

C 255 **calories** per serving

Takes **10 minutes** to prepare,
20 minutes to cook

* recommended

1 Heat a medium, non stick saucepan and spray with the cooking spray. Add the onion and ham and cook for 6–8 minutes, stirring occasionally, until the onion starts to soften, adding a little water if necessary to prevent them from sticking.

2 Pour in the lentils and drained beans, and then stir in the chilli powder to coat all the ingredients.

3 Pour in the stock and add the tomato purée. Stir well and then bring to a simmer. Continue to simmer for 20 minutes.

4 Leave to cool slightly and then remove 3–4 cups of the soup and whizz in a blender or using a hand held blender.

5 Return the blended soup to the pan and check the seasoning.

6 Serve in warmed bowls sprinkled with chopped parsley.

Variation For a vegetarian bean soup, just omit the ham. The **POINTS** values will then be 3½ per serving.

Fisherman's Catch

This soup is a substantial meal in itself, and ideal for a warming thermos flask lunch. Swirl 1 tablespoon of single cream into each soup bowl just before serving, for an extra 1 **POINTS** value per serving.

Serves 4

350 g (12 oz) skinless fish fillets, such as cod, whiting or haddock

225 g (8 oz) potatoes, peeled and cut into 1 cm (½-inch) dice

2 leeks or onions, sliced

175 g (6 oz) carrots, peeled and grated coarsely

100 g (3½ oz) frozen peas

2 tablespoons cornflour

600 ml (1 pint) semi skimmed milk

salt and freshly ground black pepper

snipped fresh chives or chopped fresh parsley, to garnish

3½ **POINTS** values per serving
13½ **POINTS** values per recipe

C   260 **calories** per serving

Takes **10 minutes** to prepare,
25 minutes to cook

✱   not recommended

1 In a large, lidded, saucepan, simmer the fish in 600 ml (1 pint) of water for 10 minutes, until tender. Drain, reserving the liquid. Flake the fish coarsely, discarding any skin and bones, and set aside.

2 Return the strained cooking liquid to the saucepan.

3 Add the potatoes, leeks or onions and carrots and simmer, covered, for 10 minutes or until the vegetables are tender. Add the peas.

4 Blend the cornflour with enough milk to make a smooth paste. Stir into the saucepan and bring to a steady boil, stirring continuously until the soup thickens.

5 Stir in the remaining milk, add the flaked fish and heat gently.

6 Season and serve in warmed bowls, garnished with the fresh herbs.

Tip Let your fishmonger know what you are cooking. There may be some tail end pieces and odds and ends of assorted fish that can be used up in a chowder. Look out for any bargain non oily fish like haddock or cod, and for added flavour, include some smoked fish.

Variations Add a teaspoon of curry paste in step 3 for a spicy fish soup, for no additional **POINTS** values.

Replace the peas with 100 g (3½ oz) baby leaf spinach, for the same **POINTS** values.

Parsnip, Ham and Apple Soup

The addition of apple gives this soup a sweet edge that enhances the intense, soothing parsnip flavour.

Serves 2

low fat cooking spray
1 large onion, chopped roughly
500 g (1lb 2 oz) parsnips, peeled and
    chopped roughly
1 cooking apple, peeled, cored and
    chopped roughly
1.5 litres (2¾ pints) vegetable stock
150 ml (¼ pint) skimmed milk or soya milk
100 g (3½ oz) lean ham, chopped
salt and freshly ground black pepper

4½ **POINTS** values per serving
8½ **POINTS** values per recipe

C   **315 calories** per serving

Takes **10 minutes** to prepare,
50 minutes to cook

✱   recommended

1 Heat a large, lidded, non stick saucepan and spray with the cooking spray. Stir fry the onion for 3 minutes, until softened and golden, adding a little water if necessary to prevent it from sticking.

2 Add the parsnips and apple and cover with the vegetable stock. Bring to the boil and then simmer for 45 minutes, covered.

3 Liquidise the soup in batches using a blender or hand held blender and return to the pan.

4 Stir in the milk. Add the chopped ham and allow to heat it through.

5 Check the seasoning and serve in warmed bowls.

Lush Lentil Soup

4 POINTS VALUE

A lovely wholesome and totally satisfying soup.

Serves 6

low fat cooking spray
1 large onion, chopped
4 garlic cloves, crushed
2 celery sticks, with leaves if possible, chopped
1 large carrot, peeled and chopped
500 g (1 lb 2 oz) red lentils
2 litres (3½ pints) vegetable stock
2 bay leaves
15 g (½ oz) porcini, soaked in 100 ml (3½ fl oz) boiling water for 10 minutes
juice of ½ a lemon
salt and freshly ground black pepper

4 **POINTS** values per serving
23 **POINTS** values per recipe

C 288 **calories** per serving

Takes **10 minutes** to prepare, **1 hour** to cook

V

✱ recommended

1 Heat a large, lidded, non stick saucepan and spray with the cooking spray. Stir fry the onion, garlic, celery and carrot for 5 minutes, until softened, adding a little water if necessary to prevent them from sticking.

2 Add the lentils, stock and bay leaves and bring to the boil. Skim off any froth that collects on the top and simmer gently, covered, for 45 minutes, until the lentils are very soft.

3 Meanwhile strain the porcini, reserving the soaking liquid, and finely chop.

4 Only after the lentils are cooked, season the soup and add the mushrooms with their strained soaking liquid.

5 Simmer for a further 5 minutes then squeeze in the lemon juice and serve in warmed bowls.

Tip To enhance the mushroom flavour, soak the porcini and then strain them through a piece of muslin or a very fine mesh strainer to remove any grit. Reserve the strained soaking liquid, finely chop the porcini, and incorporate them with the soaking liquid into your recipes to enhance the flavour of your dishes.

Manhattan Seafood Soup

A meal-in-a-bowl type of soup, this makes for a hearty lunch or light meal.

Serves 4

low fat cooking spray
2 rashers lean smoked back bacon, chopped
1 onion, chopped finely
1 green pepper, de-seeded and chopped
2 sticks celery, diced
400 g can chopped tomatoes
300 g (10½ oz) potatoes, peeled and diced
700 ml (1¼ pints) vegetable or fish stock
400 g (14 oz) frozen mixed seafood
  selection, defrosted
salt and freshly ground black pepper

3 POINTS values per serving
11 POINTS values per recipe

C **174 calories** per serving

Takes **15 minutes** to prepare,
30 minutes to cook

✱ not recommended

1 Heat a large, lidded, non stick saucepan, spray with the cooking spray and fry the bacon for 2 minutes on a high heat until lightly browned.

2 Add the onion, green pepper and celery and stir fry for 5 minutes, until beginning to soften, adding a little water if necessary to prevent them from sticking.

3 Stir in the tomatoes, potatoes and stock.

4 Season, cover, and bring to a simmer, then cook for 15–20 minutes or until the potatoes are tender.

5 Stir in the seafood and heat for 2–3 minutes.

6 Ladle into warm deep bowls or mugs to serve.

Variation Try replacing 100 ml (3½ fl oz) stock with white wine for a richer flavour. The **POINTS** values remain the same for the serving, but for the recipe they will be 12.

Chicken Noodle Soup with Coconut Milk

Transport yourself to Thailand with a bowlful of this wonderfully fragrant soup.

Serves 4

200 ml (7 fl oz) coconut milk

750 ml (1¼ pints) chicken or vegetable stock

1 teaspoon grated fresh root ginger

1 tablespoon Thai red curry paste

½ aubergine, sliced thinly

100 g (3½ oz) dried fine rice noodles

100 g (3½ oz) sugar snap peas, halved
   diagonally

300 g (10½ oz) cooked, skinless boneless
   chicken breast, torn into pieces

salt and freshly ground black pepper

2 tablespoons fresh basil leaves, to garnish

---

7 POINTS values per serving
28½ POINTS values per recipe

C **290 calories** per serving

Takes **15 minutes** to prepare,
15 minutes to cook

* not recommended

1 Pour the coconut milk and stock into a large saucepan and add the ginger and curry paste.

2 Bring to the boil, then reduce the heat and simmer for 5 minutes.

3 Add the aubergine, rice noodles and sugar snap peas. Cook gently for 4-5 minutes, then add the chicken and cook for 2–3 more minutes.

4 Season to taste and serve in warmed bowls garnished with basil leaves.

Tip Don't let any leftover coconut milk go to waste. Freeze it until you make this soup next time.

Celeriac and Crispy Bacon Soup

Celeriac is a root vegetable that tastes a little like celery. It goes perfectly with bacon, so give it a try in this lovely soup.

Serves 4

low fat cooking spray
1 onion, chopped roughly
2 garlic cloves, crushed
400 g (14 oz) potatoes, chopped roughly
2 heads celeriac, scrubbed and chopped roughly
1.2 litres (2 pints) vegetable stock
8 rashers lean back bacon, chopped
salt and freshly ground black pepper

---

4 **POINTS** values per serving
16½ **POINTS** values per recipe

C   221 **calories** per serving

Takes **15 minutes** to prepare,
35 minutes to cook

✻   recommended

1 Heat a large, non stick saucepan and spray with the cooking spray. Gently fry the onion, garlic and potatoes for 1 minute, adding a little water if necessary to prevent them from sticking.

2 Add the celeriac and stock and bring to the boil.

3 Reduce the heat and simmer for 30 minutes, or until the celeriac is tender.

4 Liquidise the soup in batches using a blender or hand held blender and return to the pan to warm through. Season to taste, remembering that the bacon will be salty.

5 Spray a non stick frying pan with the cooking spray and stir fry the bacon until crispy.

6 Serve the soup in warmed bowls with the crispy bacon sprinkled on top.

Variation You can use 400 g (14 oz) sweet potatoes instead of the potatoes, for 5 **POINTS** values per serving.

Italian Rice and Pea Soup

If you like filling, comfort food then try this classic Italian country soup. It makes the ideal all in one meal.

Serves 2

low fat cooking spray
1 small onion, chopped
2 rashers lean back bacon, trimmed and chopped
100 g (3½ oz) risotto rice
3 tablespoons white wine (optional)
750 ml (1¼ pints) hot chicken or vegetable stock
125 g (4½ oz) frozen peas
25 g (1 oz) Parmesan cheese, freshly grated
salt and freshly ground black pepper

6½ *POINTS* values per serving
13 *POINTS* values per recipe

C 380 calories per serving

Takes **5 minutes** to prepare, **25 minutes** to cook

✱ not recommended

1 Heat a large, lidded, non stick saucepan and spray with the cooking spray. Add the onion, bacon and 2 tablespoons of water to the pan, and cook until the mixture sizzles.

2 Cover the pan and cook on a medium heat for 5 minutes until the bacon and onion have softened.

3 Stir in the rice and cook for 1 minute.

4 Add the wine, if using, and cook until it has evaporated.

5 Add the stock and seasoning, and bring the mixture to the boil.

6 Reduce the heat and simmer for about 15 minutes, stirring occasionally, until the rice is tender and the soup has thickened. It should have the consistency of runny porridge.

7 Add the peas and cook for another 3 minutes. Stir in half the Parmesan cheese.

8 Serve in warmed bowls, sprinkled with the remaining Parmesan cheese.

Tip When cooking with alcohol, always boil it for a good 1–2 minutes. This ensures the flavour is less harsh.

Variation You can use 125 g (4½ oz) frozen sweetcorn instead of the peas and 4 spring onions instead of the ordinary one. The *POINTS* values will remain the same.

Brie and Courgette Soup

An unusual creamy soup that is rich and filling.

Serves 4

200 g (7 oz) potatoes, peeled and diced

300 g (10½ oz) courgettes, halved lengthways and sliced

150 g (5½ oz) leek, halved lengthways and sliced

850 ml (1½ pints) vegetable stock

½ teaspoon dried thyme

135 g (5 oz) Brie cheese, rind removed and diced

freshly ground black pepper

3½ POINTS values per serving
14 POINTS values per recipe

C 170 **calories** per serving

Takes **10 minutes** to prepare, **20 minutes** to cook

V

✱ recommended

1 Put all the ingredients, except the Brie and seasoning, into a large saucepan.

2 Bring to the boil, cover and simmer for 12–15 minutes, until the vegetables are tender.

3 Add the Brie and stir until the cheese melts – do not overcook at this stage, this should only take 1–2 minutes.

4 Liquidise the soup in batches using a blender or hand held blender and return to the pan to warm through. Season with black pepper and serve in warmed bowls.

Variation This soup can also be made by substituting mozzarella cheese for the Brie, for 3 **POINTS** values per serving.

Spicy Soups

There is no reason why soup should be boring. If you enjoy spicy food, jazz up your meals with these fabulous ideas, including Mulligatawny, Hot and Sour, Thai Spinach and Curried Lentil.

Get your tongue tingling
with a hint of spice

Spicy Prawn Broth with Noodles

The coriander garnish adds a lovely fresh taste to this zingy broth.

Serves 4

850 ml (1½ pints) fish stock
2 tablespoons soy sauce
2 red chillies, de-seeded and chopped finely
1 garlic clove, chopped
1 teaspoon caster sugar
175 g (6 oz) carrots, peeled and sliced into
  matchsticks
1 red pepper, de-seeded and sliced thinly
175 g (6 oz) tiger prawns, peeled
100 g (3½ oz) thin egg noodles
100 g (3½ oz) water chestnuts, sliced
6 spring onions, sliced
2 tablespoons chopped fresh coriander, to garnish

---

2 POINTS values per serving
7 POINTS values per recipe

C   **200 calories** per serving

Takes **10 minutes** to prepare,
10 minutes to cook

✱   not recommended

1 Place the stock, soy sauce, chillies, garlic and sugar in a large saucepan and bring to the boil.

2 Add the carrots and pepper, and simmer for 5 minutes.

3 Add the prawns to the soup along with the noodles, water chestnuts and spring onions.

4 Simmer for a further 5 minutes, stirring well to incorporate the noodles.

5 Ladle the soup into warmed bowls and garnish with the chopped coriander to serve.

Chicken and Sweetcorn Creole Soup

This tingling and spicy soup is a great introduction to using fresh chillies if you have never tried them before. Add 1 tablespoon of low fat natural yogurt per person as a delicious cooling garnish, for an additional ½ **POINTS** value per serving.

Serves 4

2 onions, quartered
2 garlic cloves or 2 teaspoons garlic purée
1 red chilli, de-seeded
1 green pepper, de-seeded
850 ml (1½ pints) hot chicken stock
100 g (3½ oz) easy cook rice
2 teaspoons ground coriander
500 g (1 lb 2 oz) chopped canned tomatoes or chunky passata
225 g (8 oz) cooked, skinless boneless chicken breast, shredded
200 g can sweetcorn kernels, drained
1 tablespoon chopped fresh oregano
salt

1 Use a blender or hand held blender to roughly chop the onions, garlic, chilli and green pepper. You could also chop them by hand but this will take longer.

2 Pour the hot stock into a large, lidded saucepan with the rice and bring to the boil.

3 Add the chopped vegetables and the ground coriander. Season with salt.

4 Cover and simmer for 10 minutes, then stir in the canned tomatoes or passata, shredded chicken, sweetcorn and oregano.

5 Cover and cook for a further 5 minutes.

6 Serve piping hot in warmed bowls.

2½ **POINTS** values per serving
10½ **POINTS** values per recipe

C 330 **calories** per serving

Takes **5 minutes** to prepare,
20 minutes to cook

✱ recommended

Spanish Bean Soup

This spicy, filling soup is so quick to make and a scrumptious meal in a bowl.

Serves 4

1 tablespoon chilli oil or vegetable oil

1 onion, chopped

1 red or green pepper, de-seeded and chopped

125 g (4½ oz) mushrooms, wiped and sliced

1 tablespoon paprika

447 g can mixed beans in spicy sauce

1 litre (1¾ pints) tomato juice

100 ml (3½ fl oz) hot vegetable stock

50 g (1¾ oz) Spanish-style chorizo or cooked continental sausage, sliced

salt and freshly ground black pepper

chopped fresh coriander or parsley, to garnish

1 Heat the chilli oil or vegetable oil in a large, non stick saucepan and sauté the onion and pepper for 3–4 minutes, until softened, adding a little water if necessary to prevent them from sticking. Add the mushrooms and paprika and cook, stirring, for 2 more minutes.

2 Tip in the beans, then add the tomato juice, vegetable stock and sliced chorizo or sausage. Bring up to the boil, then reduce the heat and simmer gently, stirring occasionally, for 5 minutes.

3 Season and serve in warmed bowls, sprinkled with chopped fresh coriander or parsley.

3½ *POINTS* values per serving
14½ *POINTS* values per recipe

C 240 calories per serving

Takes **10 minutes** to prepare, **15 minutes** to cook

✻ recommended

Variation For a vegetarian version, chop 125 g (4½ oz) cooked vegetarian sausage and add with the beans as above, for 4 *POINTS* values per serving.

Hot and Sour Soup

For a complete meal, serve this colourful soup with a 60 g (2 oz) vegetable spring roll per person, for 4½ **POINTS** values per serving.

Serves 4

1.2 litres (2 pints) chicken stock
350 g (12 oz) skinless boneless chicken breasts, sliced thinly
75 g (2¾ oz) shiitake mushrooms, halved
1 large red chilli, de-seeded and sliced
1 red or yellow pepper, de-seeded and sliced
150 g (5½ oz) pak choi, cut into quarters
100 g (3½ oz) dried egg noodles
2 tablespoons Chinese cooking wine
3 tablespoons rice vinegar
2 tablespoons light soy sauce
1½ teaspoons white pepper
fresh coriander sprigs, to garnish

2½ **POINTS** values per serving
11 **POINTS** values per recipe

C 220 calories per serving

Takes **10 minutes** to prepare, **15 minutes** to cook

✳ not recommended

1 Put the chicken stock into a large saucepan and bring to the boil.

2 Add the chicken slices, bring back to the boil and simmer for 5 minutes.

3 Add the mushrooms, chilli and pepper and bring back to a simmer. Cook for 3 minutes.

4 Add the pak choi, egg noodles, cooking wine, rice vinegar, soy sauce and white pepper.

5 Cook for a further 3 minutes until the chicken is cooked and the vegetables are tender.

6 Ladle into deep warmed bowls, garnish with coriander and serve.

Variation For a vegetarian version, use vegetable stock instead of chicken stock and replace the sliced chicken with the same quantity of sliced tofu, for 2½ **POINTS** values per serving.

Curried Lentil Soup

Split red lentils are cheap and very quick to cook. They're used here in this wonderful warming soup that is lovely and filling, but uses few **POINTS** values.

Serves 4

low fat cooking spray
1 onion, chopped
1 garlic clove, chopped
1 green pepper, de-seeded and chopped
    finely
1 large green chilli, de-seeded and chopped
    finely (optional)
1 teaspoon mild curry powder
75 g (2¾ oz) dried split red lentils
200 g can chopped tomatoes
1 litre (1¾ pints) vegetable or chicken stock
salt and freshly ground black pepper
1 tablespoon chopped fresh coriander or parsley,
    to serve (optional)

1 **POINTS** values per serving
3½ **POINTS** values per recipe

C 105 **calories** per serving

Takes **10 minutes** to prepare,
20 minutes to cook

V

✱ recommended

1 Heat a large, lidded, non stick saucepan and spray with the cooking spray. Add the onion, garlic, pepper, chilli, if using, and 4 tablespoons of water. Heat until it all starts to sizzle.

2 Stir, cover the pan and simmer for 5 minutes, stirring once half way through.

3 Add the curry powder and cook for 1 minute and then stir in the lentils, tomatoes, stock and seasoning.

4 Bring to the boil, and then reduce the heat and simmer for 12–15 minutes, until the lentils thicken and soften.

5 Check the seasoning and serve in large warmed bowls sprinkled with chopped coriander or parsley, if using.

Tip If you just want a hint of chilli, then don't cut it up – add it whole at step 3 and remove before serving.

Spicy Squash and Chick Pea Soup (1 POINTS VALUE)

A soup with an exotic hint of aromatic spices and an interesting mixture of textures.

Serves 4

low fat cooking spray
1 onion, chopped
2 garlic cloves, crushed
1 red chilli, de-seeded and diced
2 teaspoons ground cumin
1 teaspoon ground cinnamon
1 medium butternut squash, peeled, de-seeded
  and chopped small
850 ml (1½ pints) vegetable stock
400 g can chopped tomatoes
410 g can chick peas, drained and rinsed
salt and freshly ground black pepper

1 POINTS values per serving
4½ POINTS values per recipe

C **174 calories** per serving

Takes **15 minutes** to prepare,
30 minutes to cook

V

* recommended

1 Heat a large, lidded, non stick pan over a high heat and spray with the cooking spray. Fry the onion for 3–4 minutes, covered, until softened, adding a little of the stock if necessary to prevent it from sticking.

2 Stir in the garlic, chilli and spices and cook for 15 seconds over a medium heat, then mix in the butternut squash and stir to coat in the spice mixture. Add 3 tablespoons of stock, cover the pan and cook for 5 minutes over a medium heat.

3 Pour in the remaining stock, the tomatoes, half the chick peas and seasoning. Bring to the boil, cover and cook for 20 minutes or until the squash is tender.

4 Cool slightly, then liquidise the soup in batches using a blender or hand held blender. Return to the pan to warm through.

5 Stir in the remaining chick peas, adjust the seasoning and serve in warmed bowls.

Hot and Sour Prawn Soup

This soup is very quick to make and has a bite that will refresh the most jaded tastebuds.

Serves 4

450 g (1 lb) frozen, cooked, peeled prawns
zest and juice of 3 limes
4 teaspoons fish sauce
1 small green chilli, de-seeded and chopped
   finely
grated zest of 2 lemons
1 litre (1¾ pints) chicken stock
a small bunch of coriander, chopped, plus extra
   to garnish
2 shallots, chopped finely
150 g (5½ oz) shiitake or button mushrooms,
   wiped and sliced
a medium bunch of spring onions, chopped
   finely

1½ *POINTS* values per serving
6 *POINTS* values per recipe

C **135 calories** per serving

Takes **5 minutes** to prepare,
10 minutes to cook

✱ not recommended

1 Place the prawns in a bowl with half the lime juice, 2 teaspoons fish sauce, the chilli and a teaspoon of grated lemon zest. Set aside.

2 Meanwhile, place the chicken stock in a large saucepan with all the other ingredients including the remaining lime juice, fish sauce and lemon zest.

3 Bring to the boil then add the prawns and their marinade.

4 Cook for 2 minutes then serve in warmed bowls garnished with coriander leaves.

Tip Fish sauce is available in the Oriental section of most supermarkets. It is a sauce made from dried fish, which is used in many Thai and other south east Asian dishes. A good alternative is Worcestershire sauce.

Sweet Potato and Chilli Soup

This silky sweet and hot soup is just the thing for a cold wintry day.

Serves 4

low fat cooking spray
2 large onions, peeled and chopped roughly
2 garlic cloves, crushed
1–2 small red chillies, de-seeded and chopped roughly
500 g (1 lb 2 oz) sweet potatoes, peeled and chopped roughly
500 g (1 lb 2 oz) carrots, peeled and chopped roughly
1.2 litres (2 pints) vegetable stock
salt and freshly ground black pepper

1½ *POINTS* values per serving
6 *POINTS* values per recipe

C 175 **calories** per serving

Takes **5 minutes** to prepare, **25 minutes** to cook

V

✲ recommended

1 Heat a large, lidded non stick saucepan and spray with the cooking spray. Stir fry the onions and garlic until soft and golden, adding a little water if necessary to prevent them from sticking.

2 Stir in the chillies and then add the sweet potatoes and carrots. Cover all the ingredients with stock.

3 Cover the pan and bring to the boil then simmer for 20 minutes, or until the vegetables are tender.

4 Liquidise the soup in batches using a blender or hand held blender and return to the pan to warm through.

5 Season, reheat gently and adjust the consistency to your taste by adding a little water, if necessary.

6 Serve in warmed bowls or mugs.

Coconut Milk Soup with Ginger and Coriander

If you love subtle and spicy flavours, you will adore this soup and it's so simple to make.

Serves 4

low fat cooking spray
6 shallots or 1 onion, finely chopped
2 teaspoons finely grated fresh root ginger
3 tablespoons chopped fresh coriander
300 ml (½ pint) reduced fat coconut milk
1 tablespoon Thai red curry paste
425 ml (¾ pint) hot vegetable or chicken stock
1 tablespoon cornflour
250 ml (9 fl oz) skimmed milk
salt and freshly ground black pepper
coriander sprigs, to garnish

1 Heat a large saucepan and spray with the cooking spray. Sauté the shallots or onion and ginger for 2–3 minutes, until softened, adding a little water if necessary to prevent them from sticking.

2 Add the coriander, coconut milk, red curry paste and stock.

3 Bring up to the boil, then reduce the heat and simmer for 15–20 minutes.

4 Blend the cornflour with 2–3 tablespoons of the milk. Add to the saucepan with the remaining milk.

5 Bring up to the boil, stirring constantly, then reduce the heat and cook gently for 2–3 minutes. Season to taste.

6 Ladle into warmed serving bowls and garnish with fresh coriander.

4½ POINTS values per serving
18 POINTS values per recipe

C **130 calories** per serving

Takes **10 minutes** to prepare, **30 minutes** to cook

V if using vegetable stock

✱ recommended

Tip You can buy chopped 'fresh' ginger and coriander in jars, saving preparation time. Look for them in the spices section of your supermarket; you might also find them with the Oriental foods.

Curried Vegetable Soup

A warming vegetable soup that is very easy to make.

Serves 4

15 g (½ oz) low fat spread
1 onion, sliced
2 celery sticks, chopped
1 garlic clove, crushed
225 g (8 oz) mushrooms, sliced
1 litre (1¾ pints) hot vegetable stock
1 carrot, peeled and chopped

1 parsnip, chopped
2 tablespoons medium curry paste
2 tablespoons chopped fresh mint or coriander
salt and freshly ground black pepper
4 tablespoons low fat natural yogurt

1 Melt the low fat spread in a large, non stick saucepan and sauté the onion, celery and garlic for about 3 minutes, adding a little water if necessary to prevent them from sticking. Add the mushrooms and cook for 2–3 minutes.

2 Pour in the stock and bring up to the boil. Reduce the heat, add the carrot, parsnip and curry paste and cook for about 20 minutes.

3 Liquidise about half the soup using a blender or hand held blender. Return to the remaining soup in the saucepan and add 1 tablespoon of the mint or coriander. Reheat gently, then season to taste. Ladle the soup into warmed bowls and top each portion with a tablespoon of yogurt. Garnish with the remaining mint or coriander.

1½ **POINTS** values per serving
6 **POINTS** values per recipe

C 97 **calories** per serving

Takes **15 minutes** to prepare, **35 minutes** to cook

V

* recommended

Spiced Carrot Soup

Cumin seeds release a strong, pungent flavour when toasted, which means you can add an authentic, spicy taste without adding any extra **POINTS** values. Serve with 50 g (1¾ oz) of granary bread, for 1½ **POINTS** values per serving.

Serves 2

1 teaspoon cumin seeds
350 g (12 oz) carrots, peeled and diced
150 g (5½ oz) potatoes, peeled and diced
1 small onion, chopped
1 garlic clove, crushed
1 tablespoon tomato purée
600 ml (1 pint) vegetable stock
salt and freshly ground black pepper

 1 **POINTS** values per serving
1½ **POINTS** values per recipe

C 155 calories per serving

Takes **10 minutes** to prepare, **25 minutes** to cook

V

✱ recommended

1 In a small, heavy based saucepan toast the cumin seeds for 2–3 minutes over a medium heat, until you begin to smell the aroma of the spice. Remove the pan from the heat and set the cumin seeds aside.

2 Place the carrots, potatoes, onion, garlic, tomato purée and stock in a large, lidded saucepan and bring to the boil.

3 Reduce the heat, cover and simmer for 20 minutes.

4 Liquidise the soup in batches using a blender or hand held blender and return to the pan to warm through.

5 Add the toasted cumin seeds. Season to taste, stir well and heat through.

6 Ladle the soup into two warmed bowls to serve.

Tip If you prefer a chunkier soup, then don't blend it, just roughly mash it with a potato masher.

Indian Lentil Soup

Serve as a main meal soup with a medium, toasted pitta bread per person, for an extra 2½ **POINTS** values per serving.

Serves 4

100 g (3½ oz) dried red lentils, rinsed and
  drained
400 g can chopped tomatoes
1 tablespoon tomato purée
3 celery sticks, chopped
2 carrots, peeled and grated coarsely
1.2 litres (2 pints) hot vegetable stock
50 g (1¾ oz) dried long grain rice
low fat cooking spray
1 onion, chopped
1 tablespoon chopped fresh root ginger or
  1 teaspoon ground ginger
2 teaspoons ground coriander
1 teaspoon ground cumin
½ teaspoon hot chilli powder
½ teaspoon turmeric
salt and freshly ground black pepper
4 tablespoons low fat natural yogurt, to serve

2 **POINTS** values per serving
8½ **POINTS** values per recipe

C 216 calories per serving

Takes **10 minutes** to prepare,
35 minutes to cook

V

✱ recommended

1 Place the dried lentils, tomatoes, tomato purée, celery, carrots and stock in a large, lidded saucepan, bring to the boil then cover and simmer for 10 minutes.

2 Stir in the rice and simmer for a further 15 minutes.

3 Meanwhile, heat a small, non stick saucepan and spray with the cooking spray. Fry the onion until golden brown, adding a little water if necessary to prevent it from sticking.

4 Add the ginger, coriander, cumin and chilli powder and gently fry for 3–4 minutes. Stir in the turmeric.

5 Stir the onion and spices into the soup. Simmer for 5 minutes and check the seasoning.

6 Serve piping hot in warmed bowls topped with a tablespoon of yogurt.

Tip It is important to first fry ground spices before adding to other ingredients. The heat will release their natural fragrant oils and prevent an otherwise slightly bitter aftertaste and chalky feel in the mouth.

Variation This soup liquidises well if you prefer a smooth soup, but you may need to adjust the consistency by adding hot stock.

Mulligatawny Soup

Hot, spicy and warming; this tasty soup is just the thing for a chilly day..

Serves 4

1 tablespoon vegetable oil
1 onion, chopped
1 eating apple, peeled, cored and chopped
2 garlic cloves, crushed
1 parsnip, chopped
2 carrots, peeled and sliced
1 tablespoon medium curry powder
1 litre (1¾ pints) hot vegetable stock
200 g can chopped tomatoes
125 g (4½ oz) cauliflower, broken into
  small florets
125 g (4½ oz) fine green beans, sliced
2 tablespoons chopped fresh coriander, plus extra
  for garnish
salt and freshly ground black pepper
4 tablespoons low fat natural yogurt, to serve

---

1 **POINTS** values per serving
4½ **POINTS** values per recipe

C 140 calories per serving

Takes **10 minutes** to prepare,
25 minutes to cook

V

＊ recommended

1 Heat the vegetable oil in a very large, lidded, non stick saucepan and add the onion, apple and garlic. Sauté gently for 3–4 minutes, adding a little water if necessary to prevent them from sticking. Add the parsnip, carrots and curry powder. Cook gently, stirring, for a further minute.

2 Pour in the vegetable stock and tomatoes and bring up to the boil. Reduce the heat, cover and simmer gently for 10 minutes.

3 Add the cauliflower, green beans and coriander to the saucepan. Cover and simmer for a further 10 minutes, or until the vegetables are tender. Season to taste, adding a little more curry powder if you wish.

4 Serve in warmed bowls, topping each bowlful with one tablespoon of yogurt and garnishing with coriander.

Tip If you prefer a smooth soup, whizz the cooked mixture in a blender, or use a hand held blender, for 15–20 seconds.

Variation Use a mild or hot curry powder instead of medium – according to your own preferences.

Spicy Seafood Soup

This is a delicious soup for a summer day and makes a good light meal.

Serves 4

low fat cooking spray
1 onion, sliced
1 leek, sliced
1 garlic clove, chopped finely
200 ml (7 fl oz) white wine
400 g can chopped tomatoes
425 ml (¾ pint) fish or vegetable stock
1 bouquet garni
1 tablespoon fresh parsley, chopped, plus extra
  to garnish
1 tablespoon fresh dill, chopped
a pinch of cayenne pepper
½ teaspoon paprika
1 bay leaf
400 g bag of frozen seafood cocktail, defrosted
75 g (2¾ oz) cod, cut into chunks
100 g (3½ oz) mussels in their shells, scrubbed
  (see Tip)
salt and freshly ground black pepper

2 **POINTS** values per serving
8 **POINTS** values per recipe

C 194 **calories** per serving

Takes **5 minutes** to prepare,
30 minutes to cook

✳ not recommended

1 Heat a large, non stick saucepan and spray with the cooking spray. Add the onion, leek and garlic and fry gently until they are softened but not browned, about 5–8 minutes, adding a little water if necessary to prevent them from sticking.

2 Stir in the wine and reduce a little by allowing it to boil for a minute or two.

3 Add the tomatoes, stock, bouquet garni, herbs, spices and bay leaf. Bring back to simmering point. (If you like very spicy food, use up to ¼ teaspoon of cayenne pepper.)

4 Add the seafood cocktail, cod and mussels, ensuring you discard any mussels that are damaged or that remain open when tapped.

5 Heat until just simmering then reduce the heat and simmer gently, uncovered, for 10 minutes.

6 Discard any mussels that do not open during cooking. Remove the bay leaf and bouquet garni. Season to taste.

7 Ladle into warmed bowls and serve immediately, garnished with the extra parsley.

Tip To prepare mussels, scrub off any dirt and remove any barnacles. Remove the beard, if any, that sticks out between the shells. Discard any mussels that are already open or have a cracked shell.

Chilli Prawn Soup

Enjoy a delicious bowl of this spicy soup for supper with 50 g (1¾ oz) granary bread, for an additional 1½ **POINTS** values per serving.

Serves 4

1 tablespoon stir fry or vegetable oil

1 bunch spring onions, sliced finely or 1 large onion, chopped finely

1 red pepper, de-seeded and sliced finely

1 yellow pepper, de-seeded and sliced finely

1 litre (1¾ pints) hot chicken stock

2–3 teaspoons chilli sauce

1 teaspoon Chinese 5 spice powder

50 g (1¾ oz) thread egg noodles

100 g (3½ oz) prawns, defrosted if frozen

salt and freshly ground black pepper

1½ **POINTS** values per serving
6½ **POINTS** values per recipe

C 145 calories per serving

Takes **10 minutes** to prepare, **15 minutes** to cook

✱ not recommended

1 Heat the oil in a large, non stick saucepan and add the spring onions or onion and peppers. Stir fry for 2–3 minutes, adding a little water if necessary to prevent them from sticking.

2 Add the stock, chilli sauce, Chinese 5 spice powder and noodles.

3 Bring up to the boil, then simmer for 5 minutes, until the noodles are tender.

4 Add the prawns, cook for 2 minutes, then season.

5 Ladle into warmed bowls and serve at once.

Tip Stir fry oil is flavoured with garlic, ginger and spices and gives an excellent flavour to this soup, but if you don't have any you could simply use vegetable oil instead.

Variation Add the same amount of marinated tofu instead of the prawns and use vegetable stock cubes instead of chicken for a vegetarian version. The **POINTS** values per serving will remain the same.

Try using 50 g (1¾ oz) rice or small pasta shapes instead of noodles. The **POINTS** values per serving will remain the same.

Spiced Cauliflower Soup

A creamy coloured, warm and sweet, spiced cauliflower soup, especially good on dark wintery evenings.

Serves 4

1 large cauliflower, broken into florets
2 tablespoons ground cumin
low fat cooking spray
1 large onion, chopped
2 garlic cloves, crushed
1.2 litres (2 pints) vegetable or chicken stock
salt and freshly ground black pepper
a small bunch of chives, chopped, to
   garnish (optional)

0 POINTS values per serving
0 POINTS values per recipe

C **55 calories** per serving

Takes **10 minutes** to prepare,
30 minutes to cook

V if using vegetable stock

✱ recommended

1 Preheat the oven to Gas Mark 7/220°C/fan oven 200°C.

2 Place the cauliflower florets in a roasting tin, sprinkle with the cumin and seasoning and toss to coat. Spray with the cooking spray then bake for 20 minutes until tender and slightly charred.

3 Meanwhile, heat a large, non-stick saucepan and spray with the cooking spray. Stir fry the onion and garlic for 5 minutes until softened, adding a little water if necessary to prevent them from sticking.

4 Add the cauliflower to the onion and then pour the stock over. Bring to the boil and simmer for 5 minutes.

5 Liquidise the soup in batches using a blender or hand held blender and return to the pan to warm through.

6 Check the seasoning then serve in warmed bowls garnished with chopped chives, if using.

Thai Spinach Soup

A super quick and creamy soup that can be rustled up in 15 minutes. This soup can also be made with watercress instead of the spinach, for the same **POINTS** values.

Serves 4

low fat cooking spray

2.5 cm (1 inch) fresh root ginger, peeled and chopped finely

4 garlic cloves, crushed

1 teaspoon Thai curry paste

500 g (1 lb 2 oz) baby spinach or spinach, tough stems removed and leaves shredded

1.2 litres (2 pints) vegetable stock

100 ml (3½ fl oz) reduced fat coconut milk

salt and freshly ground black pepper

1 POINTS values per serving
3½ POINTS values per recipe

C **70 calories** per serving

Takes **5 minutes** to prepare, **10 minutes** to cook

V

✱ recommended

1 Heat a large, non stick saucepan and spray with the cooking spray. Stir fry the ginger, garlic and curry paste for a few minutes, until fragrant.

2 Add the spinach and stock and bring to the boil. Simmer for a few moments.

3 Liquidise the soup in batches using a blender or hand held blender and return to the pan. Stir in the coconut milk and reheat gently.

4 Check the seasoning, then serve in warmed bowls.

Tip Once you have added the coconut milk to the soup do not boil or the soup will split.

Spicy Chick Pea and Lentil Soup

A thick, warming and filling soup, with lots of nutritional goodness. Perfect for a chilly autumnal day.

Serves 6

low fat cooking spray
1 red onion, diced
2 celery sticks, diced
2 carrots, peeled and diced
1 garlic clove, crushed
50 g (1¾ oz) Puy lentils
50 g (1¾ oz) red split lentils
1 teaspoon ground cumin
½ teaspoon ground coriander
1 teaspoon grated fresh root ginger
400 g can chopped tomatoes
410 g can chick peas, drained
850 ml (1½ pints) vegetable stock
200 ml (7 fl oz) reduced fat coconut milk
salt and freshly ground black pepper

3 **POINTS** values per serving
17 **POINTS** values per recipe

C 165 **calories** per serving

Takes **15 minutes** to prepare, **15–20 minutes** to cook

V

✱ recommended

1 Heat a large, non stick saucepan and spray with the cooking spray. Add the onion, celery, carrots and garlic and cook for 2–3 minutes, adding a little water if necessary to prevent them from sticking.

2 Add the lentils and then the spices and ginger and stir well to coat the vegetables.

3 Add the chopped tomatoes and chick peas and pour in the stock.

4 Bring to the boil and simmer for 15 minutes.

5 Pour in the coconut milk and stir well.

6 Liquidise a third of the soup using a blender or hand held blender, retaining some of the chunkiness of the vegetables.

7 Return the blended soup to the pan. Stir, reheat, check the seasoning and serve in warmed bowls.

Variation For a non vegetarian version, add 50 g (1¾ oz) chopped lean back bacon when frying the vegetables, for 3½ **POINTS** values per serving.

Thai-style Carrot and Coriander Soup

This recipe is based on a vegetable soup, but with a unique twist.

Serves 4

1 litre (1¾ pints) vegetable stock
1 large onion, chopped
750 g (1 lb 10 oz) carrots, peeled and chopped
1 red chilli, de-seeded and chopped
zest and juice of a lemon
2 garlic cloves, peeled
a bunch of fresh coriander, chopped
25 g (1 oz) creamed coconut
salt and freshly ground black pepper

To garnish
fresh coriander leaves
1 red or green chilli, de-seeded and chopped
  finely, or some dried chilli flakes (optional)

1½ **POINTS** values per serving
6 **POINTS** values per recipe

C 135 calories per serving

Takes **20 minutes** to prepare,
30 minutes to cook

V

★ recommended

1 Place all the ingredients except the creamed coconut and garnish in a large saucepan.

2 Bring to the boil and then turn down the heat. Simmer for 25 minutes, until the vegetables are soft.

3 Add the creamed coconut. When the coconut has melted, liquidise the soup in batches using a blender or hand held blender and return to the pan to warm through. Taste and season.

4 Serve in warmed bowls garnished with fresh coriander and some finely chopped fresh chilli or dried chilli flakes, if using.

Variation Omit the coconut, for a zero **POINTS** value soup, or serve with 1 tablespoon of low fat natural yogurt per person, for an extra ½ **POINTS** value per serving.

Spicy Pork Meatball Soup

A wonderfully satisfying 'meal in a bowl'. The meat and stock can be prepared a day or several hours in advance.

Serves 4

4 spring onions, trimmed

2–3 small hot red chillies, de-seeded

500 g (1 lb 2 oz) pork mince

2 garlic cloves, peeled

5 cm (2 inches) fresh root ginger, peeled and cut into thin slices

4 stems lemongrass, chopped roughly

2 tablespoons coriander leaves

1.7 litres (3 pints) chicken stock

6 kaffir lime leaves or zest of a lime

2 tablespoons Thai fish sauce

low fat cooking spray

200 g (7 oz) pak choi

1 red pepper, de-seeded and sliced

4 teaspoons lemon juice

salt and freshly ground black pepper

---

4 POINTS values per serving
16 POINTS values per recipe

C **255 calories** per serving

Takes **10 minutes** to prepare, **35 minutes** to cook

✳ recommended (meatballs only)

1 Put the spring onions, chillies, pork, garlic and some salt into a blender, or use a hand held blender, with half the ginger and lemongrass. Add most of the coriander, keeping just a few leaves back as a garnish. Whizz it all together for a minute or so until it is all well combined. (If you don't have a blender, chop everything as finely as possible and knead it together with your hands in a bowl.) Wrap the mixture in clingfilm and keep in the fridge until you need it.

2 Put the chicken stock in a large saucepan and add the lime leaves or zest, fish sauce and the remaining ginger and lemongrass. Simmer for 15 minutes and then remove the ginger, lime leaves and lemongrass with a slotted spoon.

3 To make the meatballs, use wet hands to form 40 balls from the pork mixture – they need to be roughly the size of large marbles. Heat a large, non stick frying pan to a medium temperature and spray with the cooking spray. Cook the meatballs in two batches, turning them frequently as they cook. They will take about 5 minutes to brown all over.

4 Bring the flavoured stock back to the boil, season, and as each batch of meatballs is cooked, tip them into the stock.

5 Once all the meatballs are fried, stir fry the pak choi and red pepper in the frying pan, spraying with the cooking spray if needed.

6 To serve, divide the stir fried vegetables between four large warmed soup bowls and then pour the soup and meatballs over. Stir a teaspoon of lemon juice into each bowl and garnish with the remaining coriander leaves.

Variation If you can't find pak choi, you can use Chinese leaves or cabbage. The **POINTS** values will remain the same.

Suppertime Soups

Not just a quick fix for when you are feeling hungry, soups also make a delicious supper in themselves or are perfect as a starter for a supper party – try Sicilian Country Soup with Parmesan Crisps, Noodle Bar or Prawn Bisque. Or if you are feeling particuarly hungry at the end of the day but want something different, go for a filling soup such as Scotch Broth.

Impress friends and family with a delicious soup at the end of the day

Cock-a-Leekie Soup

Simmering a chicken quarter with the vegetables gives this soup a great flavour. It's inexpensive and very nourishing too.

Serves 4

135 g (4¾ oz) skinless chicken leg quarter
1.2 litres (2 pints) chicken stock
50 g (1¾ oz) dried pearl barley
1 bay leaf
2 onions, sliced
2 leeks, sliced
1 carrot, peeled and chopped
2 tablespoons chopped fresh parsley
salt and freshly ground black pepper

1½ *POINTS* values per serving
7 *POINTS* values per recipe

C **155 calories** per serving

Takes **10 minutes** to prepare,
1 hour to cook

✱ recommended

1 Put the chicken portion into a large, lidded saucepan and add the chicken stock.

2 Add the pearl barley and bay leaf, and bring up to the boil. Reduce the heat and simmer gently, partially covered, for 30 minutes.

3 Add the onions, leeks and carrot to the saucepan and continue to cook for about 20 minutes until the vegetables are tender and the pearl barley is cooked.

4 Lift the chicken portion from the saucepan, cool slightly, then remove all the meat from the bones. Chop the meat and return to the saucepan with the parsley.

5 Remove the bay leaf, reheat the soup and season to taste.

6 Ladle into warmed bowls to serve.

Mushroom and Thyme Soup

A light, full-flavoured mushroom soup that is made extra special with a touch of brandy.

Serves 4

low fat cooking spray

1 large onion, sliced

2 garlic cloves, crushed

400 g (14 oz) mushrooms e.g. field, chestnut or brown cap, sliced

3 tablespoons brandy

a small bunch of thyme, chopped, plus a few extra sprigs to garnish

600 ml (1 pint) vegetable stock

25 g (1 oz) dried porcini soaked in 600 ml (1 pint) boiling water for at least 10 minutes, chopped, soaking liquid reserved (optional)

salt and freshly ground black pepper

1 Heat a large, non stick saucepan and spray with the cooking spray. Stir fry the onion and garlic for about 5 minutes until soft, adding a little water if necessary to prevent them from sticking.

2 Add the mushrooms and stir fry over a high heat for another 5 minutes then add the brandy and cook, stirring, for 1 minute until the alcohol has evaporated.

3 Reduce the heat, add the thyme, stock, dried mushrooms, if using, seasoning and reserved soaking liquid.

4 Bring to the boil and simmer for 45 minutes.

5 Serve in warmed bowls garnished with fresh thyme sprigs.

½ *POINTS* values per serving
1½ **POINTS** values per recipe

C   55 calories per serving

Takes **10 minutes** to prepare,
1 hour to cook

V

✳ not recommended

Tip Use young thyme, sometimes known as soft thyme, as you can then use the stems as well. In older thyme you have to cut away the woody stems.

Scotch Broth

This is a soup to warm you on the coldest of days and is substantial enough for a meal. Serve with a medium slice (50 g/1¾ oz) of crusty white bread per person, for an extra 2 **POINTS** values per serving.

Serves 4

115 g (4 oz) lean lamb mince
25 g (1 oz) dried pearl barley
1 large onion, chopped finely
2 carrots, peeled and chopped finely

2 turnips, chopped
2 leeks, sliced thinly
4 tablespoons parsley, chopped
salt and freshly ground black pepper

1 Heat a large, lidded, non stick saucepan and dry fry the mince for 5 minutes, stirring frequently to break it up and lightly brown.

2 Pour in 1.2 litres (2 pints) of cold water and bring to the boil. Then use a large, shallow spoon to remove any froth that forms on the surface.

3 Reduce the heat, add the pearl barley and prepared vegetables and season.

4 Cover and leave to simmer gently for 50–60 minutes.

5 Adjust the seasoning to taste. Stir in the parsley, ladle into warmed soup bowls and serve immediately.

1½ **POINTS** values per serving
6½ **POINTS** values per recipe

119 calories per serving

Takes **10 minutes** to prepare,
1 hour to cook

∗ recommended

Sicilian Country Soup with Parmesan Crisps

In an era of TV cooks and exotic travel, let's not overlook the simply delicious fresh flavours of a country vegetable soup. Adapt this hearty soup to use your favourite, seasonal vegetables.

Serves 4

600 ml (1 pint) hot vegetable stock
1 large onion, sliced finely
1 garlic clove, crushed
1 head of fennel or 2 small fennel bulbs, outer layer(s) discarded, or 4 celery sticks, sliced finely
1 carrot, peeled and sliced finely
2 courgettes, sliced finely
2 x 400 g cans plum tomatoes
75 g (2¾ oz) spaghetti, broken into short lengths
5 cm (2-inch) strip of orange rind (optional, see Tips)
300 g can cannellini beans, drained
125 g (4½ oz) fresh or frozen spinach
1 tablespoon fresh thyme or 1 teaspoon dried thyme
50 g (1¾ oz) Parmesan cheese, grated finely
2 tablespoons chopped fresh basil
salt and freshly ground black pepper

3½ **POINTS** values per serving
14 **POINTS** values per recipe

C 235 calories per serving

Takes **25 minutes**

V

✱ recommended

1 Place the stock in a large, lidded saucepan, and bring to the boil.

2 Add the onion, garlic, fennel, carrot and courgettes to the boiling stock, cover and simmer for 10 minutes. Stir in the tomatoes, spaghetti, orange rind, if using, beans, spinach and thyme. Cover and cook for 10 minutes.

3 Meanwhile, preheat the grill to high. Using a non stick baking tray or shallow frying pan, and a plain 6 cm (2½-inch) cutter, make the cheese crisps. Place the cutter on a baking tray and sprinkle an even layer of Parmesan cheese inside the cutter, to form a disc. Repeat with the remaining cheese to make eight crisps in total. You will need to do this in two batches.

4 Place the tray under the grill to toast the cheese to a golden brown colour. This only takes a minute or so. Remove the tray and leave for a minute before carefully lifting each crisp onto a plate using a metal spatula.

5 Season the soup to taste. Stir in the basil and ladle into warmed bowls. Serve with the crisps on the side.

Tips Fennel has a distinct aniseed flavour and is a delicious but under used vegetable. Choose two smaller bulbs rather than a large one, which may have tough outer layers.

The easiest way to get a 2 inch strip of orange rind is to use a potato peeler to gently peel off some rind.

Variation A teaspoon of chilli paste will add a touch of Sicilian heat. The **POINTS** values will remain the same.

Cream of Celery and Almond Soup (3) POINTS VALUE

A very flavoursome soup and ideal for a light meal.

Serves 4

2 rashers of streaky bacon, chopped
6 celery sticks, trimmed and chopped
1 onion, chopped
1 teaspoon finely chopped fresh root ginger (optional)
600 ml (1 pint) hot vegetable stock
2 tablespoons cornflour
300 ml (½ pint) skimmed milk
25 g (1 oz) ground almonds
salt and freshly ground black pepper

To serve

4 tablespoons half fat crème fraîche
15 g (½ oz) toasted flaked almonds
celery leaves

3 *POINTS* values per serving
13 *POINTS* values per recipe

C 165 **calories** per serving

Takes **10 minutes** to prepare,
35 minutes to cook

✱ recommended

1 Dry fry the bacon in a large, lidded, non stick saucepan, cooking gently until crisp. Remove and drain on kitchen paper. Break into little bits for garnishing later.

2 Add the celery and onion to the same saucepan and sauté for 5 minutes, without browning. Add the ginger, if using, and then the stock.

3 Bring up to the boil, cover, reduce the heat and simmer for about 20 minutes.

4 Liquidise the soup in batches using a blender or hand held blender and return to the pan.

5 Blend the cornflour with 4 tablespoons of the milk. Add to the soup with the remaining milk and ground almonds.

6 Heat, stirring, until thickened, then cook gently for 2 minutes. Check the seasoning.

7 Serve the soup in warmed bowls, topped with the crème fraîche and garnished with the flaked almonds, crispy bacon bits and celery leaves.

Variation Leave out the bacon if you're cooking this soup for vegetarians and sauté the celery and onion in 3 teaspoons of butter or margarine instead, for the same *POINTS* values.

Red Pepper and Soft Cheese Soup $2\frac{1}{2}$ POINTS VALUE

This recipe is so easy. You'll be delighted with the way red peppers make such a delicious soup when combined with the creamy taste and texture of low fat soft cheese.

Serves 4

1 tablespoon low fat spread
1 large onion, chopped
2 red peppers, de-seeded and chopped
2 celery sticks, sliced
1 carrot, peeled and chopped
1 tablespoon paprika
1 litre (1¾ pints) hot vegetable stock
200 g (7 oz) low fat soft cheese with garlic and herbs
salt and freshly ground black pepper
chopped fresh coriander or parsley, to garnish

2½ **POINTS** values per serving
7 **POINTS** values per recipe

C 137 calories per serving

Takes **10 minutes** to prepare,
35 minutes to cook

V

✱ recommended

1 Melt the low fat spread in a large, non stick saucepan. Reserve a little chopped onion and red pepper and add the remainder to the saucepan with the celery and carrot.

2 Sauté gently for about 5 minutes, until softened, adding a little water if necessary to prevent them from sticking.

3 Add the paprika and cook gently, stirring constantly, for a further minute.

4 Add the vegetable stock to the saucepan. Bring up to the boil, then reduce the heat. Cover and cook over a very low heat for about 20 minutes.

5 Liquidise the soup in batches using a blender or hand held blender. Add the soft cheese and blend for about 15 seconds, until smooth.

6 Return to the pan and warm through. Season to taste.

7 Ladle the soup into warmed bowls and serve, scattered with the reserved onion and red pepper and sprinkled with chopped fresh coriander or parsley.

Tip Take time to chop the vegetables finely to enable some of the vegetables to break down during cooking and thicken the soup. This way you'll have a chunky soup that won't be too watery.

Chargrilled Aubergine Soup

Chargrilled aubergines give added depth and interest to the flavour of this unusual soup.

Serves 4

1 aubergine, sliced
low fat cooking spray
1 large onion, chopped
3 garlic cloves, crushed
175 g (6 oz) mushrooms, chopped
1.2 litres (2 pints) vegetable stock
1 tablespoon fresh coriander, chopped
½ teaspoon ground coriander
½ teaspoon ground cumin
100 g (3½ oz) low fat soft cheese
salt and freshly ground black pepper

½ *POINTS* values per serving
2½ *POINTS* values per recipe

C **76 calories** per serving

Takes **15 minutes** to prepare,
35 minutes to cook

V

✱ recommended

1 Preheat a griddle pan or the put the grill on high. Spray the aubergine slices with the cooking spray and chargrill or grill until lightly browned. Then chop roughly.

2 Heat a large, lidded, non stick saucepan and spray with the cooking spray. Cook the aubergine over a low heat with the onion, garlic and mushrooms until softened – about 3–4 minutes, adding a little water if necessary to prevent them from sticking.

3 Add the vegetable stock, fresh coriander, ground coriander and cumin. Partially cover and simmer for 15–20 minutes.

4 Add half of the soft cheese to the mixture, then liquidise the soup in batches using a blender or hand held blender. Return to the pan to warm through and season to taste.

5 Serve in warmed bowls, garnished with the remaining soft cheese and some ground pepper.

Chestnut and Mushroom Soup

This a lovely soup to make for a festive occasion. Use freshly roasted chestnuts when they are in season, otherwise use canned ones.

Serves 4

2 teaspoons vegetable oil
1 onion, chopped finely
1 carrot, peeled and chopped
350 g (12 oz) mushrooms, sliced
175 g (6 oz) peeled, roasted chestnuts (see Tip)
** or canned chestnuts**
1 litre (1¾ pints) hot vegetable stock
2 tablespoons chopped fresh parsley
100 g (3½ oz) low fat plain fromage frais
1 tablespoon cornflour
2 tablespoons medium sherry
salt and freshly ground black pepper
parsley sprigs, to garnish

1 Heat the vegetable oil in a large, lidded, non stick saucepan and sauté the onion, carrot and mushrooms until softened, about 5 minutes, adding a little water if necessary to prevent them from sticking.

2 Add the chestnuts and vegetable stock to the saucepan and bring to the boil.

3 Reduce the heat, cover and simmer for 20 minutes.

4 Transfer the soup to a blender, or use a hand held blender, and add the parsley and most of the fromage frais. Blend for about 15–20 seconds until smooth, then return to the saucepan.

5 Blend the cornflour with 2–3 tablespoons of cold water, add to the soup with the sherry and bring up to the boil, stirring constantly until thickened and smooth.

6 Taste and season the soup, then serve in warmed bowls, garnished with the reserved fromage frais and parsley sprigs.

2 *POINTS* values per serving
8½ POINTS values per recipe

C   **170 calories** per serving

Takes **10 minutes** to prepare (if using canned chestnuts), **35 minutes** to cook

V

✱   recommended

Tip To roast chestnuts, pierce them with a sharp knife on the flat side, then roast them on a baking sheet in an oven preheated to Gas Mark 6/200°C/fan oven 180°C for 15–20 minutes.

Ham, Leek and Potato Soup

This is a wonderfully wholesome soup, ideal for those 'hungry' times when you are never quite sure how many family or friends might pop by.

Serves 4

2 leeks, sliced finely

2 potatoes, peeled and sliced finely

600 ml (1 pint) hot vegetable stock

1 tablespoon cornflour

200 ml (7 fl oz) semi skimmed milk

2 teaspoons Dijon or wholegrain mustard

2 tablespoons chopped fresh parsley or 2 teaspoons dried parsley

150 g (5½ oz) wafer thin smoked ham, cut into pieces

salt and freshly ground black pepper

1 Add the leeks and potatoes to a large, lidded saucepan, pour over the hot stock, cover and cook for 10 minutes.

2 Meanwhile, blend the cornflour with the milk. Stir in the mustard and parsley.

3 Add the cornflour mixture to the potato and leeks, stirring until the mixture thickens slightly. Simmer for a further 10 minutes.

4 Add the ham to the saucepan and season to taste.

5 Heat gently for another minute or two before serving in warmed bowls.

1½ **POINTS** values per serving
7 **POINTS** values per recipe

C 145 **calories** per serving

Takes **10 minutes** to prepare, **20 minutes** to cook

✱ recommended

Variation Replace the ham with wafer thin turkey and substitute the parsley with 1 tablespoon of chopped fresh tarragon or sage. The **POINTS** values will remain the same.

Crabmeat and Prawn Wonton Soup

(2 POINTS VALUE)

Try your hand at making this light oriental-style soup – it's delicious.

Serves 4

50 g (1¾ oz) crabmeat, flaked

50 g (1¾ oz) peeled, cooked prawns, chopped finely

1 teaspoon fresh chives, chopped

12 square wonton wrappers

850 ml (1½ pints) chicken or vegetable stock

2 spring onions, chopped finely

1 bunch spinach leaves or 1 head pak choi, leaves separated

freshly ground black pepper

---

2 **POINTS** values per serving
8 **POINTS** values per recipe

C 117 **calories** per serving

Takes **20 minutes** to prepare,
5 minutes to cook

✱ not recommended

1 Mix together the crabmeat, prawns and chives.

2 Lay the wonton wrappers on a clean work surface and share the crab mixture between them, spooning it into the middle of each wrapper. Brush the edges of the wontons with a little cold water, then draw them up to form little pouches, pressing the wrappers to seal tightly.

3 For the soup, heat the chicken or vegetable stock in a large saucepan and add the spring onions and spinach or pak choi. Add the wontons and simmer over a medium heat for 3–4 minutes, or until the wontons rise to the surface.

4 Season to taste with pepper and serve at once in warmed bowls.

Tip Wonton wrappers are available from Oriental supermarkets.

Prawn Bisque

Make this easy, elegant seafood soup with frozen North Atlantic prawns for the best flavour.

Serves 4

1 onion, chopped finely
1 carrot, peeled and chopped finely
1 celery stick, chopped finely
900 ml (1¾ pints) fish stock
2 parsley sprigs, plus extra to garnish
1 bay leaf
225 g (8 oz) frozen prawns, peeled and cooked
8 tablespoons very low fat plain fromage frais
freshly ground white pepper

1½ *POINTS* values per serving
6 *POINTS* values per recipe

C **98 calories** per serving

Takes **15 minutes** to prepare,
30 minutes to cook

✳ not recommended

1 Put the onion, carrot and celery into a large saucepan with the stock. Add a couple of parsley sprigs and the bay leaf.

2 Bring up to the boil, then reduce the heat and simmer for 20 minutes until the vegetables are tender.

3 Add most of the frozen prawns, reserving a few on a covered plate to thaw out for the garnish. Cook the soup gently for 5 minutes. Remove the bay leaf and parsley sprigs.

4 Using a blender or hand held blender, liquidise the soup with half the fromage frais until smooth. Check the seasoning, adding pepper to taste (it is unlikely that you will need salt).

5 Return the soup to the saucepan and reheat gently.

6 Ladle the soup into warmed bowls and serve, garnished with the remaining fromage frais, defrosted prawns and parsley sprigs.

Tip For a super smooth texture, pass the soup through a fine sieve after blending it.

Italian Soup

You can use any type of pasta for this, including remnants from assorted half empty packets. This soup can also be served warm.

Serves 4

2 red peppers, de-seeded and chopped roughly
2 green peppers, de-seeded and chopped roughly
½ cucumber, peeled and chopped roughly
1 red onion, chopped roughly
2 garlic cloves, crushed
200 g (7 oz) cooked pasta
400 g can chopped tomatoes
2 sprigs of fresh mint or 2 teaspoons dried mint
2 tablespoons red wine vinegar
1 tablespoon sugar
salt and freshly ground black pepper

To garnish

1 yellow pepper, chopped finely
2 fresh tomatoes, skinned, de-seeded and
  chopped finely
1 pack of fresh parsley, chopped finely
ice cubes (optional)

1½ *POINTS* values per serving
5½ *POINTS* values per recipe

C 145 calories per serving

Takes **10 minutes** + chilling

V

✱ recommended

1 Whizz together the red and green peppers, cucumber, onion, garlic, pasta, tomatoes, mint, vinegar, sugar and seasoning in a blender, or use a hand held blender, for a few seconds until you have a thick soupy texture – not smooth.

2 Pour the soup into serving bowls and chill.

3 When ready to serve, garnish each bowl with some of the yellow pepper, fresh tomato, parsley and ice cubes, if using, before serving.

Tips If you do not have a blender, chop all the vegetables to a fine dice and mix with the other ingredients in a large bowl.

To skin and de-seed the tomatoes, drop them into a bowl of boiling water for 10 seconds and then remove with a slotted spoon. The skins should slip off easily. If not, then pop the tomatoes back into the boiling water for another few seconds. Cut the tomatoes into quarters and remove the seeds.

Vichyssoise

A summer classic, this soup can also be served hot, if you wish, as a leek and potato soup.

Serves 6

6 large leeks, halved and sliced thinly
low fat cooking spray
1 large onion, chopped
600 g (1 lb 5 oz) potatoes, peeled and chopped coarsely
1 litre (1¾ pints) vegetable stock
300 ml (½ pint) skimmed milk
a pinch of freshly grated nutmeg
a pinch of cayenne pepper
salt and freshly ground black pepper
fresh chives, snipped, to garnish

1½ *POINTS* values per serving
7½ *POINTS* values per recipe

C 148 calories per serving

Takes **15 minutes** to prepare,
1 hour to cook + chilling

V

✱ recommended

1 Rinse the sliced leeks and leave to drain for a few minutes.

2 Heat a large, lidded, heavy based saucepan and spray with the cooking spray. Add the leeks and onion and gently warm them through, then cover them with a piece of baking parchment tucked down the sides of the pan. Put a lid on the pan and sweat on the lowest possible heat for 25 minutes. Carefully pull the baking parchment to one side once or twice while cooking and stir gently to prevent the mixture from browning or sticking.

3 Remove the baking parchment. Add the potatoes and stock to the pan and bring to the boil.

4 Cover with the lid and gently simmer for 30 minutes until the potatoes are well cooked.

5 Liquidise the soup in batches using a blender or hand held blender and return it to the pan.

6 Stir in the milk, nutmeg and cayenne pepper. Season to taste. Leave to cool and then place in the refrigerator for several hours until well chilled.

7 Serve, garnished with the chives.

Fabulous Fish and Bean Soup

An intensely flavoured soup that's thick, rich and satisfying.

Serves 4

low fat cooking spray

1 large onion, chopped finely

4 garlic cloves, crushed

1 bay leaf

a pinch of saffron, soaked in 2 tablespoons
   boiling water (optional)

3 celery sticks, sliced finely

400 g can chopped tomatoes

400 g can red kidney beans, drained and rinsed

zest of a lemon

1 tablespoon fennel seeds

1 tablespoon tomato purée

1.2 litres (2 pints) fish or vegetable stock

500 g (1 lb 2 oz) fresh cod, or frozen and
   defrosted, skinned and cubed

a small bunch of parsley, chopped

salt and freshly ground black pepper

3 POINTS values per serving
12½ POINTS values per recipe

C   **215 calories** per serving

Takes **10 minutes** to prepare,
30 minutes to cook

✱   not recommended

1 Heat a large, lidded, non stick saucepan and spray with the cooking spray. Stir fry the onion and garlic for 5 minutes, until softened, adding a little water if necessary to prevent them from sticking.

2 Add the bay leaf, saffron and soaking water (if using), celery, tomatoes, beans, lemon zest, fennel seeds, tomato purée and stock and bring to the boil.

3 Cover and simmer for 20 minutes.

4 Add the fish to the saucepan and cook for 7–10 minutes until just cooked through.

5 Check the seasoning, then scatter with chopped parsley and serve in warmed bowls.

Broccoli Soup with Cheese Clouds

This fresh tasting soup is great to fill you up on a cold day.

Serves 4

500 g (1 lb 2 oz) broccoli, broken into florets and the stalk chopped

120 g (4½ oz) Quark

2 tablespoons skimmed milk

1 garlic clove, crushed

2 teaspoons chopped fresh herbs, plus extra to garnish

salt and freshly ground pepper

½ *POINTS* values per serving
1½ POINTS values per recipe

C **50 calories** per serving

Takes **10 minutes** to prepare, **20 minutes** to cook

V

✱ recommended

1 Bring 700 ml (1¼ pints) of water to the boil in a large, lidded saucepan, then add the broccoli. Bring back to the boil, cover the pan and simmer for 10 minutes. Remove the broccoli from the pan with a slotted spoon and put in a blender, or use a hand held blender, with a little of the cooking water. Reserve the remaining water.

2 Whizz the broccoli for 2–3 minutes, until very smooth and silky. You will need to scrape down the sides of the blender to make sure all the broccoli is processed. With the blender running, gradually pour in the remaining broccoli water. If you want a really smooth soup, strain the soup back into the saucepan through a sieve – if not, just return it to the pan. Season.

3 To make the cheese clouds, in a large bowl, beat together the Quark with the skimmed milk until you have a soft, dropping consistency. Mix in the garlic and herbs.

4 Reheat the soup gently and pour into warmed bowls. Drop small dollops of the cheese mixture to float on top of the soup and serve at once, sprinkled with chopped herbs.

Tip For a zero *POINTS* value soup, simply leave out the cheese clouds.

Noodle Bar Soup

Imagine yourself sitting in a noodle bar enjoying this very tasty Oriental soup. The stock is packed full of vegetables and a little shredded cooked chicken, yet it certainly fills you up. To make it more substantial, add 50 g (1¾ oz) of cooked spaghetti or crushed vermicelli, for an extra ½ **POINTS** values.

Serves 1

300 ml (½ pint) chicken stock

20 g (¾ oz) carrots, peeled and sliced very thinly

20 g (¾ oz) green beans or mange tout, topped, tailed and halved

30 g (1¼ oz) cooked, skinless, boneless chicken breast, shredded

1 tablespoon soy sauce

3 fresh coriander sprigs, chopped, to serve

½ **POINTS** values per serving
½ **POINTS** values per recipe

C **60 calories** per serving

Takes **5 minutes** to prepare,
5 minutes to cook

✱ recommended

1 Bring the stock to the boil in a large saucepan.

2 Add the carrots and simmer for 2 minutes.

3 Add the green beans or mange tout, chicken and soy sauce and simmer for a further 2 minutes.

4 Serve in deep warmed bowls scattered with the coriander leaves.

Beetroot and Crème Fraîche Soup

This luxurious soup is simplicity itself to make but impressive enough to serve to guests.

Serves 4

low fat cooking spray

4 shallots or 2 onions, peeled and chopped

2 x 100g (3½ oz) potatoes, peeled and chopped

1 kg (2 lb 4 oz) vacuum packed cooked beetroot, drained and chopped

1.2 litres (2 pints) vegetable stock

150 g (5½ oz) reduced fat crème fraîche

salt and freshly ground black pepper

a small bunch of chives, chopped, to garnish (optional)

2½ **POINTS** values per serving
9½ **POINTS** values per recipe

C 235 **calories** per serving

Takes **10 minutes** to prepare,
20 minutes to cook

V

✱ recommended

1 Heat a large, lidded, non stick saucepan and spray with the cooking spray. Stir fry the shallots or onions and potatoes for 5 minutes, until golden, adding a little water if necessary to prevent them from sticking.

2 Add the beetroot and stock and stir together, then cover and bring to the boil. Simmer gently for 15 minutes.

3 Liquidise the soup in batches using a blender or hand held blender and return to the pan, but do not reheat.

4 Check the seasoning and then add the crème fraîche and swirl together rather than mixing it in fully.

5 Serve in warmed bowls garnished with chives, if using.

Tip If reheating this soup be careful not to boil as it may split.

Cream of Chicken Soup

Comforting and delicious, who can resist a piping hot bowlful of chicken soup?

Serves 4

1 tablespoon low fat spread
1 onion, chopped finely
1 leek, sliced finely
3 celery sticks, chopped
1 parsnip, chopped
250 g (9 oz) chicken leg quarter, skinned
1.2 litres (2 pints) hot chicken or vegetable stock
100 g (3½ oz) very low fat plain fromage frais
2 tablespoons chopped fresh parsley
salt and freshly ground black pepper

3 POINTS values per serving
11 POINTS values per recipe

C **121 calories** per serving

Takes **10 minutes** to prepare,
45 minutes to cook

★ recommended

1 Melt the low fat spread in a large, non stick saucepan and gently sauté the onion, leek, celery and parsnip until softened, for about 10 minutes, adding a little water if necessary to prevent them from sticking.

2 Add the chicken to the saucepan with the hot stock. Bring to the boil and then reduce the heat. Cover and simmer gently for 30 minutes.

3 Using a slotted spoon, lift the chicken from the saucepan and put it on a chopping board. Let it cool down for a few minutes and then use two forks to strip off all the meat, discarding the bones.

4 Transfer the soup to a blender, or use a hand held blender, adding half the chicken and all the fromage frais. Whizz for about 15–20 seconds until smooth.

5 Return the soup to the saucepan, add the parsley and remaining chicken and reheat gently. Season to taste, ladle into warmed bowls and serve at once.

Variation To make a cream of vegetable soup, omit the chicken and use vegetable stock cubes. Add a couple of chopped carrots to the saucepan and sauté them with the other vegetables, for 1 **POINTS** value per serving

French Onion Soup

(3) POINTS VALUE

Filling and fabulous – with deliciously cheesy croûtons.

Serves 4

low fat cooking spray
600 g (1 lb 5 oz) onions, sliced very finely
1 teaspoon caster sugar
1 tablespoon plain flour
1.5 litres (2¾ pints) hot vegetable stock
150 ml (¼ pint) dry white wine
8 x 2.5 cm (1-inch) thick slices of French stick
60 g (2 oz) reduced fat mature Cheddar cheese, grated
salt and freshly ground black pepper

---

3 POINTS values per serving
11½ POINTS values per recipe

C **206 calories** per serving

🕐 Takes **10 minutes** to prepare, **40 minutes** to cook

V

✱ not recommended

1 Heat a large, lidded saucepan and spray with the cooking spray. Add the onions, sprinkle with the sugar and sauté for 20 minutes, stirring frequently to remove any caramelized onions off the bottom of the pan.

2 Season, add the flour and cook, stirring, for a few minutes.

3 Add the hot stock, more seasoning and the wine and continue stirring with a wooden spoon to prevent the mixture from sticking to the bottom of the pan. Bring to the boil.

4 Reduce the heat, cover and simmer for 15 minutes. Meanwhile, preheat the grill to high.

5 Toast the bread slices on one side, then turn and place, toasted sides down, on a baking sheet and cover each slice with grated cheese. Grill for 2–3 minutes until the cheese is bubbling and golden.

6 Pour the hot soup into warmed soup bowls or a large, warmed tureen. Float the croûtons on top, then serve.

Parsnip and Pear Soup

A real autumnal treat, this mixture of parsnips and pears is simply delicious.

Serves 4

low fat cooking spray
2 onions, chopped
2 garlic cloves, crushed
750 g (1 lb 10 oz) parsnips, scrubbed and chopped roughly
1 pear, cored and chopped roughly
1.2 litres (2 pints) vegetable stock
salt and freshly ground black pepper

1 Heat a large, lidded, non stick saucepan and spray with the cooking spray. Gently stir fry the onions and garlic with 4 tablespoons of water until softened.

2 Add the parsnips, pear and stock, cover the pan and bring to the boil.

3 Turn down the heat and leave to simmer for 20 minutes, or until the parsnips are soft.

4 Liquidise the soup in batches using a blender or hand held blender and return to the pan to warm through. Season to taste.

5 Serve in warmed bowls with freshly ground black pepper on top.

2 *POINTS* values per serving
8½ **POINTS** values per recipe

C 172 **calories** per serving

Takes **20 minutes** to prepare, **30 minutes** to cook

V

✴ recommended

Tip For soups like this that are liquidised after cooking, you don't need to peel the vegetables. Fruit and vegetables that are not peeled are worth more nutritionally, as many of the vitamins and minerals are found just below the skin.

Variation Try using a Cox apple in place of the pear. The *POINTS* values per serving will remain the same.

Roasted Tomato and Red Pepper Soup with Garlic Croûtes

Full of flavour, this is an easier soup than it might appear as most of the cooking is done in the oven.

Serves 4

6 tomatoes, skinned (see Tip on
  p144) and halved
3 red peppers, de-seeded and cut
  into quarters
garlic low fat cooking spray

4 thin slices (2½ cm/1 inch thick)
  of French bread or 8 thin slices
  of French baguettine
450 ml (16 fl oz) vegetable stock

1 Preheat the oven to Gas Mark 6/200°C/fan oven 180°C. Place the tomatoes and red peppers on a baking tray and spray with the cooking spray. Roast for 40 minutes. Remove the baking tray from the oven. Transfer the tomatoes, pepper and any juices to a blender, or use a hand held blender, and whizz until smooth.

2 Spray a clean baking tray with the cooking spray and place the slices of French bread on it. Spray the bread with the cooking spray and cook in the oven for 3–5 minutes, until starting to brown and crisp.

3 Meanwhile, mix together the liquidised vegetables and stock and warm through in a saucepan. To serve, ladle the soup into warmed bowls and top with a croûte or croûtes.

1 *POINTS* values per serving
4 *POINTS* values per recipe

C 100 calories per serving

Takes 10 minutes to prepare,
45 minutes to cook

V

* recommended (soup)

Index